P9-DFR-897

PRESERVING

OUR

ITALIAN

HERITAGE

A Cookbook
Sons of Italy Florida Foundation

The Grand Lodge of Florida, Order Sons of Italy in America, Inc. and the Sons of Italy Florida Foundation created a non-profit trust in 1988. The purpose of this trust is for charitable, cultural, literary, educational, scientific or medical research.

The proceeds from the sale of this book will be used by the Sons of Italy Florida Foundation for the purpose of this trust, a perpetual scholarship program and for charities. We appreciate your support of our Fraternal Organization.

Preserving Our Italian Heritage Cookbook placed second in the 1991 National TABASCO® Community Awards Cookbook competition. The award was presented by Paul C.P. McIlhenny, Vice President of McIlhenny Company, before the annual conference of The American Institute of Wine and Food in New Orleans, Louisiana.

Additional copies may be obtained at the cost of $14.95 per book, plus $3.00 postage and handling. Send to:

Sons of Italy Florida Foundation
87 NE 44 Street #5
Fort Lauderdale, Florida 33334

Allow 2-3 weeks delivery.

Printed in the USA by

WIMMER
The Wimmer Companies, Inc.
Memphis

"Preserving Our Italian Heritage" is more than just a cookbook. It is a collection of recipes from the hearts and minds of our forefathers, many handed down from generation to generation and written down for the very first time in this book.

Over 500 recipes were received from the members of the Grand Lodge of Florida. A few were received on notepaper, just jotted down. Some in yellowed envelopes written by a family member long departed. Some precious old recipes that called for "half an eggshell full" or "add a wine glass of". All, family tested favorites and traditional holiday recipes.

As we compiled, we felt a sense of urgency to record all the marvelous recipes from the different regions of Italy. We have included many familiar foods, some similar, some so different that you will feel compelled to try the recipe.

These wonderful foods are nostalgic and heart-warming, evoking beautiful memories of the past, entwining and reaching out to today.

We hope you enjoy our cookbook and you will find in its pages a special recipe that will become a family favorite.

It is also our hope that some day, somewhere, someone will read our cookbook and quietly sigh "Thank you for taking the time to write it all down". We feel this cookbook is truly a reflection of our cultural heritage.

Rose Marie Boniello, Editor

COOKBOOK COMMITTEE

Chairman:	Rose Marie Boniello
Editor and Title:	Rose Marie Boniello
Assistant Editors:	Lucy Yonnetti Gladys Marino
Word Processing:	Lucy Yonnetti Tina Piasio
Type Setting:	Patricia McDougle
Proffers:	Antonette Zaffarano Dora Battaglia Renata Curcio Rathmann Fortune Bosco
Publicity:	Gladys Marino

IN MEMORIUM

Sales and Distribution:	*M. Plama Guarante*
Co-Chairman/Proofer:	*Olga Clementi*

A special thanks to the artists who donated their time and expertise for the cover art and divider illustrations.

Cover Art Direction and Design:	Kevin A. McDonagh
Cover Illustration:	James DeBarros
Illustration Photographed by:	George DuBose
Divider Illustrations by:	Dolores G. Russo

Expression of Appreciation

This cookbook is the culmination of many long hours of dedicated work and through its medium we are sharing some truly treasured recipes.

We would like to thank all the Lodge members who contributed their time and recipes. We also thank those whose faith in this project made it all come true.

Finally, we as co-chairmen, have at last seen our dream become a reality in the publication of this book.

Rose Marie Boniello
Olga Clementi

We regret that all recipes submitted could not be used. To ensure consistency of form, liberties may have been taken with original recipes.

CONTENTS

ANTIPASTI/ APPETIZERS

Italian Sausage Pie

1 pie shell
  (can use pizza dough)
3/4 lb. sweet sausage
  (remove casing/crumble)
1/2 cup onions

3 eggs, beaten
1/2 cup milk or cream
1 cup cheese, shredded
  (mozzarella or provolone)
salt/pepper

Place dough in pie pan. Saute sausage and onions, drain, and spoon into prepared pie pan. Blend eggs, cream, cheese, salt and pepper pour over sausage and bake until custard forms. Bake in 350 degree oven 35 minutes. Allow to cool. Serve in small pieces.

Flo Carbone
Sunrise-Tamarac Lodge #2542
Helen Carelli
John Paul I Lodge #2427

Pepperoni Pie

2 cups pepperoni, chopped
2 cups milk
2 eggs, beaten

1/2 lb. mozzarella, cubed
1 1/2 cups flour

Mix all ingredients well and pour into greased 9"X 11" pan. Bake at 400 degrees for 30 minutes or until set.

Origin: "Cousin" Brenda Orio

Marie Scarpelli
Sunrise-Tamarac Lodge #2542

Artichoke Pie

1 pkg. artichoke hearts, frozen
4 eggs
1/2 cup pepperoni, diced

1 cup mozzarella, shredded
1/2 cup grated cheese
1-9" pie shell

Cook artichokes, drain and cut. Beat eggs thoroughly and add all ingredients. Mix well and pour into 9" pie shell. Bake at 375 degrees for 45-60 minutes. May be frozen after baked. Serve as part of antipasto or as a first course.

Mary Ahles
John Paul I Lodge #2427

Pepper Biscuits

6 cups flour	1 1/2 tsp. black pepper
6 tsp. baking powder	(coarse grind)
1 1/4 cup vegetable oil	2 tsp. salt
1 1/2 cups white or red wine	warm water as needed
	(about 1/4 cup)

Mix in order given - knead about 15 minutes. Take a small amount of dough (size of small walnut), shape in finger twist or knot and place on ungreased cookie sheet. Bake 375 degrees 15-20 minutes until brown. Serve with cocktails. Can be frozen.

**Florence Santi
John Paul I Lodge #2427**

Bagna Cauda
(Hot Anchovy Dip)

1/2 pound butter	6 tbsp. olive oil
6 garlic cloves, crushed	1 tsp. black pepper
2 oz. can anchovies	artichokes/raw vegetables

Combine butter, olive oil, black pepper and anchovies. Cook on low heat 10 minutes until the anchovies have disintegrated. Pour into a Fondue Pot or chafing dish, to keep warm. Surround with slices of artichokes and raw vegetables. Any leftover Bagna Cauda may be used as sauce on pasta. *Traditionally served in a clay pot.*

**Lillian Ferrari Menza
Joseph Franzalia Lodge #2422**

Stuffed Clams

2 cans minced clams	2 tsp. lemon juice
1/4 lb. butter	1 tsp. oregano
1 onion, chopped fine	2 green bell peppers
bread crumbs	(chopped fine)
Jarlsberg cheese, grated	hot pepper sauce, optional

Simmer clams, lemon juice, oregano and butter in saucepan for 15 minutes. Add hot pepper sauce, bread crumbs, onion and green peppers, until mixture is the consistency of oatmeal. Fill clam shells with mixture and top with grated Jarlsberg. Bake in 325 degree oven for 15-20 minutes until mixture starts to bubble. Serves 10-12.

Origin: Aunt Helen Scarpelli

**Lucy Yonnetti
Sgt. F. M. Bonanno Lodge #2549**

Ostriche All' Italiana
(Baked Oysters with Bread Crumbs)

2 tbsp. butter
1 tsp. garlic, finely chopped
2 tbsp. parsley, finely chopped
3 tbsp. Parmesan cheese, grated
2 tbsp. butter, cut in pieces

1 cup fresh bread crumbs
(3 slices Italian bread)
2 doz. fresh oysters shucked
(may use frozen)

In a heavy skillet melt 2 tablespoons of butter over moderate heat. When foam subsides, add bread crumbs, and garlic. Toss 2-3 minutes until crisp and golden. Stir in parsley and grated cheese. Sprinkle crumbs on oysters. Dot the top with tiny bits of butter. Bake in shallow pan, large enough to hold oysters in a single layer.

Preheat oven 450 degrees. Bake oysters in top third of oven for 12-15 minutes until the crumbs are golden. Juices in the dish should be bubbling. Serve at once as an antipasto or first course.

Maria Cellucci Atkins
Key West Lodge #2436

Baked Mussels

3 doz. mussels

1/2 cup crushed tomatoes

Bread crumb stuffing:

2 cups bread crumbs
4 tbsp. grated cheese

3 garlic cloves, diced
2 tbsp. parsley, chopped

Scrub mussels with a brush, pull off beards. Prepare a fry pan with a tight fitting lid that will hold all the mussels. Add 3-4 tbsp. olive oil, 1/3 cup water, salt and pepper. Cover pan, let mussels steam over medium heat to open. Remove mussels to cool and reserve liquid. *Do not use unopened mussels.* Remove mussels and open shells to lay flat. Do not break apart. Place one mussel in each shell, cover mussels with prepared stuffing. Squeeze 1 tbsp. of crushed tomatoes on each mussel. Sprinkle with chopped parsley. Drizzle with olive oil and remining liquid from steam process to moisten bread crumbs.

Bake 375 degrees until golden brown - about 15-20 minutes. Serve hot.

Rose Marie Boniello
Sgt. F. M. Bonanno Lodge #2549

Eggplant Caponata
(Poor Man's Caviar)

1 eggplant, unpeeled & cubed
1/4 cup green pepper
4 oz. can mushrooms and stems
   (drained)
1/3 cup olive oil
salt / pepper
1/4 cup water
1/4 cup capers

1 medium onion, chopped
1/4 cup celery, chopped
2 garlic cloves, minced
6 oz. can tomato paste
1/2 tsp. oregano
1/2 cup stuffed green olives
2 tbsp. wine vinegar or
   (cider vinegar)

Combine all ingredients. Pour into a 2 quart glass casserole, cover with lid. Mix well and microwave for 10-12 minutes. Stir again and microwave a few minutes more until eggplant is tender. Serve as appetizer on crackers, chips or Italian bread cut thin.

Gloria Macari
John Paul I Lodge #2427

Eggplant Caponata

1 large eggplant
2 1/2 cups onions, sliced
2 cups Marinara sauce
2 tbsp. sugar
1/2 tsp. salt
12 pitted green olives, sliced

1/2 cup olive oil
1 cup celery, diced
1/4 cup wine vinegar
2 tbsp. capers, drained
dash of pepper
toast rounds

Wash eggplant, cut 1/2" cubes. In skillet, saute eggplant in 1/2 cup olive oil until tender and golden brown. Remove eggplant and set aside.

In same skillet, add 2 tablespoons of oil and saute onion and celery until tender, about 5 minutes. Return eggplant to skillet, stir in tomato sauce, bring to boil. Reduce heat and simmer covered for 15 minutes. Add vinegar, sugar, capers, salt, pepper and olives simmer covered stirring occasionally for an additional 20 minutes.

Cover eggplant, refrigerate overnight. To serve - turn mixture into serving bowl and surround with toasted rounds. Serves 6-8.

Laura Spoto
La Nuova Sicilia Lodge #1251

Eggplant Caponata

2 eggplants	2 tsp. salt
1/2 cup olive oil	2 onions
16 oz. can Italian tomatoes	3 celery stalks
1/2 cup pitted green olives,	3 tbsp. capers
chopped	1/4 tsp. basil
1/4 cup wine vinegar	4 tbsp. sugar
1 garlic clove	salt/pepper

Cut eggplant into 1" cubes. Sprinkle with salt and let stand in colander about 2 hours. Squeeze gently. Saute eggplant in oil until brown on all sides. Remove from pan with slotted spoon. Brown chopped onions until soft, add tomatoes, celery and olives cook slowly until celery is tender. Return eggplants to pan, add capers. Heat vinegar, add sugar and dissolve. Pour mixture over eggplants, add garlic, basil, salt and pepper. Cover and simmer about 20 minutes stirring occasionally. Serve hot or cold.

Carmela Cannata
Unita Lodge #2015

Variation

6 medium Zucchini, in place of eggplants
Omit basil and green olives.

Lena Piasecki
Unita Lodge #2015

Eggplant Caponata

6 eggplants, small cubes with skin	2 large onions, small pieces
1 bunch celery, diced/parboiled	1 lb. large pitted green olives
1 large can crushed tomatoes	(small pieces)
1 tbsp. sugar	4 oz. white wine
oil to fry	

Put eggplant in pot and sprinkle with salt. Stir occasionally and let sit for 2 hours. Drain eggplant, squeeze to remove excess water. Saute eggplant in 3 tbsp. oil until tender. (Add oil as needed) Remove from pan and set aside. Add 3 tbsp. oil to pan, saute onions slightly, add tomatoes. Simmer about 30 minutes. Add sugar, wine, eggplants, celery and olives. Stir and simmer 5 minutes. Let cool and refrigerate. Serve cold as appetizer with bread or crackers.

Origin: Sicily, Italy

Dora Battaglia
Lake Worth/Boynton Beach Lodge #2304

Caponata Sicilian Style I

1 large eggplant, unpeeled
1 green pepper, chopped
1 celery stalk, chopped (parboiled)
1 large onion, chopped
1 can tomato sauce
1/2 cup olive oil
1 tbsp. parsley, chopped

1 tbsp. oregano
2 tbsp. capers
2 tbsp. vinegar
1 tbsp. sugar
1/2 jar stuffed green olives
(with pimentoes, sliced)

Cut eggplants into small squares. Do not peel or overcook. Fry in olive oil, remove and set aside. In same oil, fry the pepper and onion, set aside. Boil the olives 1-2 minutes to remove bitterness, Combine all ingredients in frying pan, add celery, and tomato sauce. Simmer for 10 minutes. Add salt and pepper to taste. Serves 4.

Virginia A. Papale
Sunrise-Tamarac Lodge #2542

Caponata Sicilian Style II

4 medium eggplants
1 1/2 cups olive oil
4 onions, sliced
1/2 cup tomato sauce
4 celery stalks, diced
1/2 cup capers

12 green olives, pitted and cut
1 tbsp. pine nuts
1/2 cup wine vinegar
1/4 cup sugar
3/4 tsp. salt
1/2 tsp. pepper

Peel and dice eggplants and fry in 1 cup of olive oil. Remove fried eggplant from skillet, add remaining oil and onions and brown gently. Add tomato sauce and celery then cook until celery is tender, adding a little water, if necessary. Add capers, olives, pine nuts and fried eggplant. Heat vinegar in small saucepan, dissolve sugar in vinegar and pour over eggplant. Add salt and pepper then simmer 20 minutes, stirring frequently. Cool before serving. This caponata will keep in the refrigerator for a long time.

Rose A. Malzone
Fort Lauderdale Lodge #2263

Caponatina

1 large eggplant	1 cup celery, diced
1 large onion, sliced thin	1/2 cup black or green olives
3 tbsp. capers	(pitted and sliced)
1/2 cup wine vinegar	2 tbsp. sugar
salt	1 cup tomato puree or
	(Marinara Sauce)

Peel and dice eggplant, sprinkle lightly with salt and place in a colander weighted down with a heavy plate. Let stand 2 hours; water will drain. Pat pieces dry with paper towel. Simmer celery in unsalted water for 10 minutes. Reserve celery and water.

Fry diced eggplant in 1 cup of oil, gently brown. Remove eggplant from skillet and add sliced onion, gently brown. Add remaining celery, capers, olives, pine nuts, fried eggplant, tomato puree or sauce.

Heat vinegar in small saucepan, dissolve sugar in vinegar and pour over eggplant add salt and pepper and simmer for 20 minutes, stirring frequently. Cool before serving.

Alfa Rosso
Sgt. F. M. Bonanno Lodge #2549

Stuffed Mushroons

1 lb. large mushrooms	1/2 tsp. salt
1/3 cup olive oil	1/2 tsp. pepper
2 garlic cloves	3/4 cup bread crumbs
1 tsp. parsley	grated cheese (optional)

Cut off stems and wash well. Chop stems saute in olive oil with garlic a few minutes; add bread crumbs and brown. Remove from stove.
Add parsley, salt, pepper and cheese. Mix well. Fill each cap with teaspoon of bread mixture until all is used. Place on oiled cookie sheet. Bake in hot oven 400 degrees - 15-20 minutes.

Theresa Crissifulli
John Paul I Lodge #2427

Funghi Alla Trapanese
(Trapani-style Stuffed Mushrooms)

18 medium-size mushrooms
3 garlic cloves, finely chopped
1/2 cup olive oil
1 egg, beaten
1/2 cup grated Parmesan cheese
1/4 cup parsley, chopped
1 lemon

1 onion, finely chopped
6 anchovy fillets, chopped
salt / pepper
1/2 cup fresh bread crumbs
  (trim crust, soak in milk)
1/3 cup fine dry bread crumbs

Wipe the mushrooms clean with a cloth, but *Do Not Wash* them. Cut off and chop the stems. Combine onion, garlic, anchovies and mushroom stems in skillet. Add half the oil and cook over medium-high heat for 10 minutes, stirring. Remove from heat and season with salt and pepper.

Let the mixture cool, then add the egg, bread, parmesan cheese, and parsley and stir with a wooden spoon until well blended. Fill the mushroom caps with this mixture and sprinkle with the bread crumbs.

Preheat oven to 350 degrees. Brush a little oil on the bottom of baking pan and arrange mushrooms in it. Sprinkle with remaining oil and bake until crumbs are golden, about 20 minutes. Squeeze a few drops of lemon juice over each and serve. Serves 6.

H. Guy Graziani
Joseph Franzalia Lodge #2422

Cavolfiore con Uovo
(Cauliflower with Egg Batter)

1 large cauliflower
2 cups flour

2 cups olive oil
3 eggs, well beaten

Boil cauliflower until tender. *Do Not Overcook.* When cooked, cool and cut in medium pieces. Dip in flour and eggs, then fry pieces in hot oil until golden brown. Serves 5.

Cauliflower can be served as a vegetable with meats or as appetizer.

Ellen C. (DiNardo) Feigenbaum
Fort Lauderdale Lodge #2263

Spinach Appetizer

2 boxes frozen spinach, chopped
2 cups bread crumbs
1 large onion, chopped fine
3 oz. Romano cheese

4 eggs, beaten
3/4 cup melted butter or
   margarine
salt / pepper

Thaw and drain spinach, do not cook. Mix bread crumbs with spinach; add all ingredients. Chill in refrigerator. When cold, form into 1" balls. Bake on ungreased cookie sheet for about 20 minutes at 375 degrees. Drain on paper towels. Roll balls in Romano cheese while hot. Makes about 40 appetizers.

Mary Anne Ricci
Justin Antonin Scalia Lodge #2235

Cardoni Fritti

3 eggs, beaten
1 tbsp. parsley
salt/pepper
2 tsp. garlic, minced

1 bunch of cardoons
2 cups bread crumbs
oil for frying

Trim thistle-like leaves from cardoon, wash and scrape with a potato peeler to remove the grainy outer skin. Cut cardoon in pieces about 4" long. Boil in water until tender. Drain and pat dry with paper towel. Combine eggs, parsley, garlic, salt and pepper in bowl. Dip cardoon pieces in egg, then in bread crumbs. Fry in oil until golden brown.

Millie McCarthy
Federico Tesio Lodge #2619

Our family serves the cardoon fritti as an appetizer with a glass of wine.

Dora Battaglia
Lake Worth/Boynton Beach Lodge #2304

Red Roasted Pepper Antipasto

4-6 fresh firm red bell peppers   **Olive oil**
salt / pepper

Place oven temperature on broil.

Wipe peppers clean with paper towels. Place whole pepper on broiler pan lined with aluminum foil, place on rack at broil level. Turn peppers often until skins are blistered and blackened. Remove from oven. Place peppers in a clean paper bag, closed tightly to cool. Working over a bowl to catch juices, peel skins and remove seeds. Cut peppers into strips, add olive oil, salt, pepper and pepper juices. Toss lightly, store tightly covered in refrigerator. Serve on your favorite cracker or bread.

Origin: Old Family Recipe

Angie Terrana
Unita Lodge #2015

Variation

1 tbsp. fresh garlic, minced
1 tbsp. fresh broad leaf parsley, chopped fine

Add above ingredients to peppers, juice, olive oil, salt and pepper. Toss lightly to blend flavors.

When yellow peppers are in season, I broil red, green and yellow peppers for a colorful appetizer.

Origin: My Mother-In-Law, Rosina Boniello

Rose Marie Boniello
Sgt. F. M. Bonanno Lodge #2549

Variation

Add to roasted peppers, cut wedges of plum tomatoes, fresh basil chopped, chopped garlic (optional)

Antonette Zaffarano
Sgt. F. M. Bonanno Lodge #2549

Mozzarella Cheese in Carrozza
(Served with Anchovy Sauce)

8 slices Italian bread
8 oz. mozzarella cheese
salt / pepper

1/2 cup milk
2 eggs, beaten
4 tbsp. butter

Trim crusts from bread. Divide mozzarella cheese into 4 thick slices; place each slice on a slice of bread. Cover with a second slice of bread. Beat milk and eggs together in a bowl. Dip sandwiches in egg mixture. Melt butter in skillet. Saute sandwiches over medium heat until lightly browned on both sides. Add more butter during cooking if needed. Cut each sandwich in sections. Serve with Anchovy Sauce, if desired. Serves 4.

Anchovy Sauce

2 tbsp. butter
1 garlic clove, minced
1 (2oz.) can anchovy fillets
pepper to taste

3 tbsp. olive oil
2 tbsp, parsley, chopped
1 tsp. sweet basil, chopped

Saute garlic in butter and oil simmer for 5 minutes. Drain oil from anchovies into saucepan. Chop anchovies; add to saucepan with parsley and basil. Simmer for 5 minutes. Season with pepper. Do not add salt to this recipe. It has a salty flavor.

Marie LoSapio
Mike Accardi Lodge #2441
Margaret Scarfia
John Paul I Lodge #2427

Polpette di Patate e Tonno
(Potato and Tuna Appetizer)

1 potato
4 celery stalks, leaves only
   (chopped)
1 egg, beaten

1/2 onion, diced
1 can tuna

Boil potato and mash. Add leaves of 4 stalks of celery, 1/2 onion diced and 1 can of tuna. Mix well, shape in balls, dip in egg and fry.

Renata Curcio Rathmann
La Nuova Sicilia Lodge #1251

Polpo con Salsa de Aceto
(Octopus with Vinegar Sauce)

1 Octopus about 2 lbs., cleaned
15 leaves fresh mint, chopped
1/4 cup wine vinegar
1 tsp. sugar

4 large garlic cloves, chopped
1/4 cup olive oil
1/8 cup water

Boil octopus whole for 25 minutes, rinse under cold water rubbing off as much skin as possible. Slice entire octopus in small pieces, set aside in serving bowl.

Mix vinegar, water, sugar and mint, set aside. Saute garlic in olive oil to a golden color, let cool, then pour in vinegar mixture, cover the pot. Bring to boil and remove from heat. Pour over octopus, mix well and refrigerate for 2 hours before serving.

Antonette Zaffarano
Sgt. F. M. Bonanno Lodge #2549

Pickled Zucchini Appetizer

4 lbs. small zucchini,
   (sliced, 1/4" thick)
Parmesan grated cheese
bread crumbs

1/2 cup mint leaves, chopped
red wine vinegar, as needed
   (to sprinkle on each layer)
olive/vegetable oil

Use oval serving platter, sprinkle with vinegar. Fry zucchini slices in oil until brown. Place single layer in dish. Sprinkle with mint leaves, grating cheese, and vinegar. Sprinkle bread crumbs lightly on top. Repeat in layers. Refrigerate - take out 2 hours prior to serving. Serve with crackers.

When the zucchini is plentiful, we make it in a crock. A treat to serve unexpected company".

Origin: Enna City, Italy

Jack Calabro
Key West Lodge #2436

Vinegar Peppers

Wipe 4 to 6 green bell peppers clean, do not wash, cut in half, remove seeds and cut into slices. Place slices in a heated glass jar with sliced onions and or peeled garlic cloves. Bring to boil wine vinegar diluted with water. Pour this over the peppers, push peppers down with a wooden spoon to remove any air bubbles. Seal jar well. Place in refrigerator or a cool dry place to cure 4-6 weeks. Peppers are crunchy and delicious. Use vinegar peppers in an appetizer salad or with eggs for a frittata. Vinegar peppers are especially good when combined with sausage and onions.

(To preserve vinegar peppers in a larger quantity)

Wipe clean (do not wash) whole green and red peppers with the stems on. Pack into a large stone crock. Toss in whole garlic clove (peeled to the last thin skin). Bring to a boil red wine vinegar and dilute with water. Pour over the peppers to cover. On top of peppers place a wooden lid that fits snugly inside the crock. Put weight on top (clean bricks) to hold pepper under vinegar. Cure 4-6 weeks. Peppers should be crunchy. Store in a cool dry place.

My father's recipe - as a young girl I helped my father make wine, cure capocollo, preserve vinegar peppers, wrap apples in newspapers and put carrots, celery, cabbage and potatoes in the raised sand floor of our dirt cellar.

Rose Marie Boniello
Sgt. F. M. Bonanno Lodge #2549

Easy Pickled Eggplant

1 small eggplant (1 lb.)	1 qt. screw top jar
2/3 cup wine vinegar	4 garlic cloves, quartered
2 hot green peppers	Olive oil

Wash, pare and slice eggplant very thin, then cut into thin strips. Place eggplant strips into jar and set aside. Slice green peppers crosswise. Combine vinegar, garlic cloves and green peppers. Pour this mixture over eggplant in the jar. Cover the entire mixture and eggplant with olive oil. Screw the cap on the jar and shake the jar several times to properly mix the jar contents. Refrigerate the jar for at least 24 hours; open the jar and enjoy your pickled eggplant.

Jean Boniello
Sgt. F. M. Bonanno Lodge #2549

Pickled Eggplant

2 large eggplants	2 garlic cloves, chopped
4 tbsp. salt	1 tbsp. oregano
1 cup water	Pinch of cayenne pepper
1/4 cup white distilled vinegar	1 cup olive oil

Peel eggplant and slice into finger length pieces approximately 1/4" thick. Place in a large container, sprinkle with salt and water. Let stand for 2 hours weighted down with a plate. Squeeze and wring out all excess moisture from the eggplant using hands. Rinse in cold water and squeeze water out several times.

Place in clean bowl and add oil, vinegar, chopped garlic, oregano and cayenne. Taste and salt if necessary. It should be a little salty. Place eggplant in jars and cover with olive oil. Close jar tightly. Store for 2 weeks before eating - makes 1 quart.

Rose Marie Tufarella
Sunrise-Tamarac Lodge #2542

De Carlo's Eggplant Marinade

1 eggplant (1 lb)	3 garlic cloves, sliced
1/2 tsp. oregano	1/2 fresh green pepper
1 tsp. parsley	(without seeds)
1 tsp. basil	1/2 fresh red pepper
1 tsp. mixed spices	(without seeds)
1/3 cup olive oil	2/3 cup wine vinegar

Set out 1 quart size, screw-top jar. Wash, pare eggplant; slice very thin. Arrange slices in large bowl with some sprinkling of salt on each round.

Cover bowl with plastic paper and put a plate on top of plastic paper and weigh it down with a heavy object to get the water out of the eggplant. Let stand about 3 hours. When ready, squeeze eggplants and cut slices into strips. Place into large bowl. Add seasonings and diced fresh peppers. Mix well. Add vinegar and olive oil. Mix again. If more seasoning needed, season to taste.

Put mixture into quart, screw-top jar. Store in refrigerator, at least 24 hours before serving. Serve cold.

AnnMarie DeCarlo-Sides
Veto J. Presutti Lodge #2463

Long Hot Green Peppers
(Stuffed with salted anchovies)

Wipe peppers with paper toweling, do not wash. Remove stem and seeds being careful not to break the pepper. Work with rubber gloves.

Stuff each raw pepper with a whole anchovy that has been wiped of excess salt. (It is not necessary to remove soft center bones).

Push peppers into a clean sterilized jar that is long enough to fit the longest pepper. Push and gently bend as many peppers as you can possibly fit very tightly in this jar.

Fill with olive oil, moving peppers gently to let air bubbles escape. Cover tightly and let cure in the refrigerator 6-8 weeks.

Delicious as an appetizer cut into 1" circles with crusty bread.

For a hearty lunch, place one long pepper between 2 slices of firm Italian bread. With a glass of red wine and some black olives, it becomes a lunch to truly enjoy in the ways of our grandfathers.

Family Favorite.

**Rose Marie Boniello
Sgt. F. M. Bonanno Lodge #2549**

Pickled Mushrooms

1-2 lbs. mushrooms	12 garlic cloves, sliced
white vinegar	2 tsp. red pepper flakes
1/2 tsp. salt	2 tsp. capers
Olive oil	

Mushrooms: Select button mushrooms. If unavailable, slice medium-sized mushrooms in half.

Wash mushrooms, place in a deep fry pan, cover with vinegar and bring to a boil. Drain in a colander, cool. Toss mushrooms with garlic, red pepper, capers and salt. Pack into a glass quart jar, then fill with oil. Use a long knife to gently release air pockets. Refrigerate.

I also pickle cauliflower, sliced green bell peppers and cubed eggplant with this recipe.

**Esther Leucci
Sgt. F. M. Bonanno Lodge #2549**

MINESTRE/
SOUPS

Escarole, Beans and Pork Ribs Soup

2 lbs. escarole
2 cans cannellini beans
  (undrained)
1 large onion, chopped
2 tbsp. tomato paste, optional
salt/pepper

2 lbs. pork ribs, country style
2 qts. chicken broth
1 tbsp. olive oil
garlic powder, optional
red pepper, optional

Use a large pot, coat with olive oil and lightly brown pork ribs, add chopped onions saute together. Add broth, tomato paste and seasonings, cook for one hour. Wash and cut escarole in large pieces, cook for 3 minutes in boiling water, drain but reserve some water. Add escarole and beans to rib soup. If extra liquid is needed, add from boiled escarole and stir together, simmer for a few minutes.

Serve hot with Italian bread. Serves 8.

Origin: Mother-in-law who had 11 children to feed.

Ann Cavalluzzo
Ft. Lauderdale Lodge #2263

Risi e Bisi
(Venetian Rice and Pea Soup)

3 tbsp. onions, chopped
1 (10 oz.) pkg. peas, frozen
6 cups chicken broth
3 tbsp. parsley, chopped

6 tbsp. butter
1/2 tsp. salt
1 cup rice, uncooked
2/3 cup grated Parmesan cheese

In large saucepan or Dutch oven, saute onion in butter until golden. Add peas and salt, cook for two minutes, stirring often. Add broth. Bring to a boil, add rice, stirring thoroughly. Simmer for an additional 25 minutes or until rice is tender. Add parsley. Remove from heat. Add Parmesan cheese just before serving. Serves 6.

Renata Curcio Rathmann
La Nuova Sicilia Lodge #1251

Zuppa di Lenticchie alla Paesana
(Lentil Soup)

1 lb. lentils	8 cups water
1 large carrot, cut bite size	1 stalk celery, cut bite size
1/4 cup onion, chopped	2 garlic cloves, minced
1 1/2 cups canned tomatoes	1/2 tsp. marjoram
(crushed)	1 or 2 links Italian sausage

If desired, cook elbow pasta al dente and add to soup.

Rinse lentils, place in a soup kettle, cover with 8 cups of water. Let come to a boil. Cut sausage in pieces and add to lentils, cook slowly for 45 minutes. In separate pan saute garlic, onion, celery and carrot in olive oil, add salt, pepper, chopped tomatoes and marjoram. Cook for about 20 minutes and add to the lentils and simmer altogether 10 minutes longer, until lentils are tender.

Alba Bevino
Joseph A. Franzalia Lodge #2422

Variation: Omit garlic and marjoram and add 1 bay leaf. Use 2-3 fresh tomatoes, peeled, seeded and chopped in place of canned tomatoes. Serve with Parmesan cheese. May add diced cooked ham to the soup before serving. Serves 6-8.

Vinnie Fragala
Township Sons of Italy #2624

Soup Palermo Style

1/2 lb. dried kidney beans	1/2 lb. dried chestnuts
(or lentils)	(shelled)
1 stalk celery, diced	1 small onion, chopped
1 cup uncooked rice, washed	4 tbsp. olive oil
salt/pepper	

Soak beans and chestnuts overnight, drain. Place in large kettle with 3 quarts of cold water, add celery and onions. Simmer until beans and chestnuts are soft (about 1 1/2 hours). Add rice, oil and seasonings. Stirring constantly with a wooden spoon, cook until rice is tender (about 20 minutes). If necessary, add more water. Serve immediately. Serves 4.

Origin: Old family favorite

Angie Terrana
Unita Lodge #2015

Stracciatella con Pasta
(Roman Egg Soup)

4 cups chicken broth
4 eggs
1 1/2 tbsp. Parmesan cheese
1 tbsp. parsley, chopped

1 cup cooked noodles
1 1/2 tbsp. semolina or flour
salt/pepper

Place chicken broth in a soup kettle. Bring to a slow boil. Add cooked noodles to broth and boil gently. Beat eggs in a bowl until thick. Combine with flour, cheese, salt and pepper. Stir a little broth into eggs. Slowly pour the egg mixture into simmering broth, stirring gently. Continue to stir, simmer for five minutes. Top with parsley. Serves 4.

Note: To cook noodles, heat 3 cups of water and 1 tablespoon salt, when water is boiling, add one cup noodles. Simmer until tender. Drain.

Renata Curcio Rathmann
La Nuova Sicilia Lodge #1251

Zuppa di Cipolle con Uova
(Onion Soup with Eggs)

1/4 cup olive oil
3-4 fresh ripe tomatoes, chopped
3-4 cups water
Parmesan cheese
Friselle or dry toast Italian Bread

2 large sweet onions
  (sliced thin)
4-8 large eggs
salt/pepper

Saute onions until light golden brown and soft texture. Add tomatoes, salt and pepper. Simmer about 5-10 minutes, stir occasionally, add water and simmer another 5 minutes. Break eggs, slide into onion mixture and let poach. Place Friselle or Italian bread in soup plates, serve one or two eggs on each plate. Ladle onion soup over all. Sprinkle with cheese. Serves 4 for a quick lunch.

Suzy Vargas
Sgt. F. M. Bonanno Lodge #2549

Zuppa di Sposalizio
(Italian Wedding Soup)

Chicken Broth
1 3-lb. soup chicken
1 small onion

2 tbsp. salt
6 qts. water

Meatballs
1 lb. ground chuck
1 garlic clove
1/4 cup water
2 tbsp. parsley

1 cup bread crumbs
1 small onion
2 eggs

Chop garlic, onion and parsley very fine and add to other ingredients. Mix well and form into very small meatballs.

Prepare
3 cups cooked, chopped escarole or endive
1/2 cup Romano cheese mixed with 2 eggs

Boil chicken, salt and onion in water until tender. Do not overcook. Remove chicken from broth. Chill broth and skim fat. Debone chicken, remove the skin and cut into small pieces. Set aside. Return broth to heat; boil rapidly, drop in meatballs, lower heat and cook about 15 minutes. Add chicken pieces and escarole. Cook 10 minutes more, then add cheese and egg mixture while soup is boiling, cook an additional 5 minutes. Serve hot!

My mom usually made this as our first course when we had company.

Gloria (Scalzitti) Walker
Joseph A. Franzalia Lodge #2422

Soup Squares

6 eggs
1/2 cup grated Parmesan cheese
garlic powder

bread crumbs
2 tbsp. parsley, chopped fine
salt/pepper

Beat eggs with a fork, add cheese, parsley and spices then add enough bread crumbs to make a loose mixture. Pour into a greased cookie sheet. Bake 12 minutes in a 350 degree oven - cut into squares like croutons 1" x 1". Float in hot soup.

Origin: Bari

Jeanette D'Alessandro
Coral Springs Lodge #2332

Genovese Rice and Bean Soup

1 lb. green cabbage, chopped
2 med. onions, chopped fine
2 med. potatoes, peeled and diced
6 cups water
1/4 tsp. pepper
1/2 cup brown rice
salt/pepper

1/2 lb. fresh spinach
  (stemmed and chopped)
2 tbsp. olive oil
1 tsp. salt
1 can white beans, drained
1-2 tbsp. Pesto sauce

In a large sauce pan, combine the cabbage, spinach, potatoes, onion and oil with rice and the 6 cups of water. Bring to a boil, add salt and pepper and simmer for about an hour. Add canned beans and continue to simmer 10 minutes longer. Remove from heat, stir in pesto and allow to stand for at least 10 minutes before serving. Soup is often served at room temperature, at which point it will be thick and stew-like.

Lee Myers
Joseph A. Franzalia Lodge #2422

Minestrone

1/2 cup olive oil
3-4 sprigs of parsley, chopped
1/4 head of cabbage, shredded
1/4 lb. green beans, cut 1" pieces
2 cups beef broth
1 or 2 cans kidney beans
  (or cannellini beans)
1 cup onions, chopped

1 garlic clove, chopped
3 stalks celery, diced
3 carrots, sliced
1 can tomato paste
9 cups water
3 small zucchini, chopped
1 cup tubitini or elbow pasta
salt/pepper

Heat olive oil, saute onions, garlic, parsley, celery, cabbage, carrots, and green beans until wilted. Add tomato paste, beef broth, salt, pepper and water and simmer 45 minutes. Add beans, zucchini and pasta, cook 15 minutes more until pasta is al dente. Pass the Parmesan cheese.

Claire Lessa
Submitted by Edythe Dell'Orfano
Sunrise-Tamarac Lodge #2542

Minestrone Calabrese

1 lb. beet greens	2 qts. water
4 tbsp. olive oil	1 tsp. salt
1/3 lb. fresh pork rind	2 tsp. parsley
(cut in 1" pieces)	1/4 tsp. pepper
1/4 lb. prosciutto, cut small	1/2 lb. spaghetti
3/4 lb. cannellini beans	(broken in 1" pieces)
1 small zucchini, diced	1 cup Parmesan cheese

Wash beet greens and chop coarsely. Heat oil over medium heat, add pork rind, onion and parsley, cook slowly. Add prosciutto, beans and water, season with salt and pepper, cover and simmer for 1 1/2 hours. Add beet greens. When soup starts to boil add pasta. When pasta is al dente add zucchini. The finished soup should be thick. Serve with grated Parmesan cheese. Serves 6.

Origin: My Grandmother

Virginia A. Papale
Sunrise-Tamarac Lodge #2542

Zuppa di Vongole
(Baby Clam Soup)

4 1/2 - 5 lbs. baby clams	1 lb. ripe tomatoes, peeled
1/2 cup olive oil	(coarsely chopped)
2 garlic cloves, chopped	pepper
2-3 sprigs parsley	toasted Italian bread
(finely chopped)	

Wash and scrub the clams and soak them in cold salted water. Add handful of oatmeal, let stand for 30 minutes to allow any remaining sand to fall to bottom of bowl. Rinse thoroughly in a colander under running water.

Heat oil, saute garlic and parsley over low heat for 2 minutes. Add tomatoes, season with salt. Raise the heat to moderate and cook for 15 minutes. Add clams, cover the pan, lower heat again and cook for 10 minutes or until the shells have opened. Sprinkle with fresh ground pepper. Serve immediately, poured over slices of toast in individual soup bowls. Serves 6.

Mary P. Ricci
Justin Antonin Scalia Lodge #2235

Zuppa di Scarola
(Escarole Soup)

1/2 cup vermicelli (1 1/2" pieces) 1 head escarole (bite-sized pieces)	2 tbsp. carrots, chopped 2 qt. chicken broth salt/pepper 8 tbsp. Parmesan cheese

Cook vermicelli less than al dente, drain. Simmer escarole and carrot in chicken broth seasoned with salt for 20 minutes. Add the pasta and simmer for another 3 minutes. Add black pepper, stir well. Ladle into hot soup bowls. Pass Parmesan cheese, Serves 4.

Mary P. Ricci
Justin Antonin Scalia Lodge #2235

Zuppa di Cozze
(Mussel Soup - Taranto Style)

1/4 cup olive oil 4 lbs. mussels, scrubbed 1 1/4 cup dry white wine	2 large garlic cloves, crushed 1/4 cup parsley, chopped 8 slices Italian bread

Heat oil over medium heat in large frying pan, add garlic and brown, being careful not to burn. Remove garlic, add mussels and shake them around in pan. The minute the first mussel opens add parsley and the wine. Wine must cook long enough to loose its alcoholic content (about 4 minutes). Do not overcook. Discard mussels that have not opened.

Meanwhile toast bread, rub with raw garlic, then put the bread in large warm soup plates. When the mussels have all opened, portion them out among the soup plates and pour on the pan juices. Serve the zuppa hot.

In Taranto, mussels are cultivated and are among the best in the world. Most of the natives enjoy eating them raw with a squeeze of fresh lemon and a piece of crusty Italian bread.

Origin: Taranto from the Province of Puglia

Antonette Zaffarano
Sgt. F. M. Bonanno Lodge #2549

Mamma's Lentil Soup

1 lb. lentils	2 tbsp. olive oil
4 cups chicken broth	2 garlic cloves, minced
3 cups water	4 carrots, diced

In a large soup pot bring lentils, broth and water to a boil and simmer for 1 hour and 15 minutes.

In a small pan, gently saute garlic in olive oil until golden brown. Add to cooking lentils with carrots. Simmer for 30 minutes more or until lentils are very tender.

Serve with grated cheese and hot Italian bread. Serves 8-10.

Option: Add 1/2 lb. cooked ditalini or spaghetti broken into 2" pieces.

Nancy Carastro
Unita Lodge #2015

Clam Soup alla Siciliana

40 little neck clams	1 tbsp. tomato paste
1/2 cup olive oil	1/2 cup warm water
1 garlic clove	1/2 tsp. salt
3 anchovy fillets, chopped	1/2 tsp. pepper
1 tbsp. parsley, chopped	1/4 tsp. oregano
1/2 cup dry wine (red)	8 thin slices Italian bread
	(fried in olive oil)

Wash clams and scrub shells well with vegetable brush. Place oil in large saucepan, add garlic, brown and remove. Add anchovies, parsley and wine to oil and cook about 5 minutes. Add tomato paste, water, salt and pepper then cook for another 5 minutes. Add clams, cover pan and cook until all the shells are open. Add oregano and cook 2 minutes longer. Place 2 slices fried bread in each soup dish. Serve a portion of clams and juice into each dish.

Origin: This was my Mom's recipe

Helen P. Mirabole
Unita Lodge #2015

Chicken Soup ✭

1/2 chicken, cut in pieces
3 stalks celery, diced
1/2 can tomatoes, crushed
grated Parmesan cheese

2 carrots, diced
2 garlic cloves
1/4 lb. pasta or rice
(partially cooked)

Place all ingredients, except pasta, in a stock pot, cover with water, bring to a boil and boil gently for about 1 1/2 hours partially covered. When chicken is fork tender, remove from broth. Strain soup broth reserving vegetables. Place all vegetables in a blender and liquify. Return to broth. Remove skin and bones from chicken, cut into small pieces and return to broth. Bring soup back to a boil, add pasta or rice and simmer 5 minutes to finish cooking. Serve soup with grated cheese. Serves 2.

Dora Battaglia
Lake Worth/Boynton Beach Lodge #2304

Beef Soup

1 lb. chuck steak or soup meat
2 stalks celery, diced
1/2 can tomatoes, crushed
salt/pepper
1 onion, sliced
wine vinegar

3 carrots, diced
1 onion, chopped
1/4 lb. small pasta or rice
(cooked very firm)
olive oil
grated Parmesan cheese

Place meat, carrots, celery, onion, salt, pepper and tomatoes in a stock pot, cover with water and bring to boil. Lower heat and gently boil, partially covered for 1 1/2 hours until meat is very tender. Remove meat and strain broth reserving vegetables. Place vegetables in a blender and liquify, return to broth. Bring broth to boil and add pasta or rice, simmer 2-3 minutes until cooked. Serve and pass the grated cheese.

Soup Meat Salad
Cut or shred soup meat and place in a serving bowl with sliced onion. Drizzle oil and wine vinegar over top and toss. Adjust seasoning and serve with soup and salad. Serves 2.

Dora Battaglia
Lake Worth/Boynton Beach Lodge #2304

Sicilian Escarole and Sausage Soup ⚔

1 lb. sweet and hot sausage (remove casings)	3 tbsp. olive oil
1 large onion, sliced	3 garlic cloves, minced
2 qts. chicken broth	3 carrots, sliced
1 bunch parsley, chopped	2 heads escarole, cut-up
4 leaves fresh basil, chopped	1 tbsp. rosemary
	1-2 tsp. oregano

In large pot, heat oil, brown garlic and sausage thoroughly. Add onions and carrots. Saute for 5 minutes. Add broth, escarole, parsley, rosemary, basil and oregano, stir well. Bring to a boil, lower heat and simmer for 1 hour. Serve with crusty hot Italian bread and grated Parmesan cheese. Serves 10-12.

Origin: Family favorite.

Russell R. Russo
Sgt. F. M. Bonanno Lodge #2549

Italian Sausage Soup with Tortellini

1 lb. Italian sausage	1 cup onion, chopped coarsely
2 garlic cloves, sliced	5 cups beef broth
1/2 cup water	1/2 cup dry red wine or water
4 medium tomatoes (peeled, seeded, chopped)	1 cup carrots, thinly sliced
1/2 tsp. oregano	1/2 tsp. basil
8 ozs. tomato sauce	1 1/2 cups zucchini, sliced
3 tbsp. fresh parsley, chopped	8 ozs. frozen tortellini (meat or cheese)
1 medium green pepper (cut in 1/2" pieces)	grated Parmesan cheese

Remove sausage from casing then brown in 5 qt. dutch oven. Remove sausage; drain, reserving 1 tablespoon of the drippings in dutch oven. Saute onions and garlic in drippings until onions are tender. Add beef broth, water, wine, tomatoes, carrots, basil, oregano, tomato sauce, bring to a boil. Reduce heat; simmer uncovered 30 minutes. Skim fat from soup. Stir zucchini, tortellini, parsley and green pepper. Simmer covered an additional 35-40 minutes or until tortellini are tender. Sprinkle Parmesan cheese on top of each serving. Makes 8 servings.

Origin: Family favorite

Tana Lynn Boniello Mitchell
Sgt. F. M. Bonanno Lodge #2549

Brodo di Pasta e Fagioli con Polpettine
(Pasta and Bean Soup with Meatballs)

1/2 lb. dried cannellini
(or navy beans)
1/4 lb. salt pork, diced fine
5 garlic cloves, mashed
3 tsp. salt
2 tsp. crushed red pepper
1 tsp. oregano
1-16 oz. can tomatoes, crushed
1/2 cup carrots, julienned
1 egg
1/2 lb. Ditalini

1/2 lb. dried kidney beans
1/4 cup olive oil
1 large onion, chopped fine
4 celery stalks with leaves
(sliced thin)
1 tsp. black pepper
1 tsp. basil
fresh parsley, snipped
1/2 lb. ground sirloin
4 tbsp. seasoned bread crumbs
grated Parmesan cheese

Rinse and pick over the dry beans and soak overnight. Drain, then place in stockpot with 10 cups of cold water. Bring to boil, reduce heat to simmer while preparing vegetables.

Combine the ground meat, egg and bread crumbs. Roll into miniature balls, set aside. Heat olive oil in a heavy skillet over medium heat. Add salt pork and cook, stirring about 15 minutes until lightly brown. Do not allow to burn. Add onion and garlic, saute gently until the onion is golden. Add this mixture to the beans, together with celery, salt, red and black pepper, oregano and basil. Cover and simmer until beans are tender, about 2 1/2 hours.

Check frequently, if necessary add more water (there should be enough liquid to cook the meatballs and pasta in the last half hour of cooking stage). During last 1/2 hour add tomatoes, undrained and parsley. Add meatballs and carrots to the simmering soup. Cook 20 minutes then add ditalini and cook until tender. Serve with grated cheese. Makes 8 servings.

Rose Malzone
Ft. Lauderdale Lodge #2263

Pane e Pizze/
Bread and Pizza

Focaccia

2 cups tepid water
2 pkgs. rapid-rise yeast
5 1/2 cups flour
1/2 cup olive oil
1 tsp. salt

rosemary leaves
chopped garlic
coarse salt
4 tbsp. olive oil

Combine water and yeast. Set aside to bubble up and foam. Place flour in a pot large enough to hold dough that will double in size. When yeast has foamed, gently add olive oil. Pour over flour, mix and knead until dough forms. Cover and set aside. When double in size (about 2 1/2 hours), knead dough down. Let rise a second time. Cut dough in half. Flour a board and roll dough out onto two baking sheets. Brush with olive oil, sprinkle rosemary leaves, chopped garlic and coarse salt over top. Bake 375 degree for 30 minutes.

Origin: Rose Peppe, Bari, Italy

**Marie Abbate
Lake Worth/Boynton Beach Lodge #2304**

Piadina
(Griddle Flat Bread)

3 cups flour
3 tbsp. shortening
1 tbsp. salt

2 tsp. baking powder
pinch of baking soda
l cup ice water

Mix all together to form a dough. Cut into 4 or 5 pieces. Roll out thin to about an 8" circle. Prick top with a fork and bake in a hot oiled griddle or skillet. Turn with a spatula, being careful not to burn (cooks fast). Very good to eat with sauteed greens such as escarole. This recipe makes about four or five 8" to 10" Piadinas.

Origin: Republic San Morino, Italy

**Florence Santi
John Paul I Lodge #2427**

Sausage Bread

1 1/2 lbs sausage
  (remove from casing)
8 oz. mozzarella, cubed
1/2 cup grated parmesan
1 lb. pizza or bread dough

2 eggs
1/4 tsp. oregano
2 tsp. parsley
salt/pepper

Cook sausage in frying pan and drain. In a large bowl, combine sausage, mozzarella, parmesan, 1 whole egg and egg white. Mix well. Add parsley, oregano, salt and pepper. Roll dough into a pizza circle. Spread sausage mixture on top to within 1" of the edge. Roll up dough like a jelly roll shape, put on cookie sheet. Brush top lightly with beaten egg yolk. Bake 350 degrees for 45 minutes or until golden brown.

Origin: Lee Pesci

Connie Agliardi
Jerry Barletta Lodge #2502
Elvira Pezzolla
Sgt. F.M. Bonanno Lodge #2549

✕ 90 Minute Bread

2 cups water
  (slightly warmer than lukewarm)
2 packets of dry yeast
1 tsp. salt

1 tbsp. sugar
3 tbsp. corn oil
4-4 1/2 cups bread flour

Pour water into bowl and sprinkle yeast over it. Sprinkle sugar and salt over yeast and wait until yeast bubbles and comes to the surface. Stir in oil. Add 4 cups of flour all at once. Mix with a wooden spoon until dough gathers together into a ball. Scrape down sides of bowl incorporating dough particles. If dough is sticky, add additional flour until it can be handled easily. Turn dough out onto floured bread board and divide into two loaves. Shape each loaf and place into greased bread pans and cover with a dish towel. When bread has doubled in bulk, bake 375 degrees in preheated oven for 30-35 minutes until brown. Turn on to a rack to cool.

Origin: Catherine McCormick

Marie Lotito
Rev. Albert B. Palombo Lodge #2512

Pagnotta
(Sweet Raisin Bread)

4 pkg. yeast
1 cup lukewarm water
1 tsp. sugar
7 cups flour
1 1/2 cups raisins
4 tbsp. olive oil

6 large eggs, room temperature
1 1/2 cups sugar
1 oz. anise flavoring
1 lemon rind, grated
1 orange rind, grated
dash of salt

In a large bowl, dissolve yeast and sugar in lukewarm water. When yeast has foamed, add the eggs and sugar that have been beaten together. Add anise, grated rinds, and salt. In a large pot, mix flour and raisins. Add yeast mixture to four, mixing and blending to form a dough. Rub oil over dough and set covered out of draft to rise. In about 2 hours, punch dough down and let rise again. (Oil your hands before handling dough so it doesn't stick). On second rise, divide dough into four pieces. Shape into loaves and place into 4 oiled bread loaf pans. Let rise to double in bulk. Bake at 350 degrees 10 minutes. Loosely cover pans with foil, reduce heat to 300 degrees and bake 20 minutes longer.

Florence Santi
John Paul I Lodge #2427

Pepperoni Bread

1 lb. bread dough (fresh or frozen)
6 oz. pepperoni, chopped
8 oz. mozzarella, chopped
2 tbsp. oil
1/4 cup flour

Raise dough. Roll out on floured board to size of medium pizza. Spread pepperoni and mozzarella evenly to 1" border. Roll up dough like a jelly roll. Curve to form a horseshoe shape. Grease a round pan and place dough on pan, brush top and sides lightly with oil. Bake at 350 degrees in preheated oven for 30 to 40 minutes until golden brown.

Tina Piasio
Lake Worth/Boynton Beach Lodge #2304

Pizza

Pizza Dough

3 cups flour
3 tbsp. salad oil
1 egg

l tbsp. salt
1 pkg. dry yeast
1 cup lukewarm water

Dissolve yeast in lukewarm water. Place flour on board and make a well. Add ingredients to flour and mix well with fingers. Knead thoroughly to form a smooth ball of dough. Rub dough with oil, place in a bowl and cover. Set in a warm place until dough has doubled in bulk. Roll out dough to fit a baking sheet.

Pizza Sauce

1 lb. can plum tomatoes, crushed
1 garlic clove

3 tbsp. salad oil
l tsp. oregano

Brown garlic and oil, remove garlic. Add plum tomatoes and simmer 25-30 minutes.

Cover prepared dough with your favorite topping.

Tomato and Cheese Pizza

Pour a generous layer of sauce over dough. Sprinkle one cup grated parmesan cheese, 4 oz. mozzarella cheese (shredded) and one tsp. of oregano over top. Drizzle with olive oil.

Sausage Pizza

Cover dough with 2 cups of tomato sauce, spread 1/2 lb. cooked sausage (crumbled) and 1 cup of grated parmesan cheese over top.

Anchovy Pizza: **No Tomato Sauce.**

Cut 10 anchovies into small pieces. Place on dough. Sprinkle with olive oil, 1 tsp. oregano and 1/2 cup pitted black olives.

Bake in a hot oven, 400 degrees, for 25-30 minutes or until dough is golden brown. Serve immediately.

Origin: My Mom's recipe.

Rose Malzone
Ft. Lauderdale Lodge #2263

Focaccia Ripieno
(Stuffed Flat Bread)

5 cups flour
1 cup warm water
1 tsp. salt

1 pkg dried yeast
1/4 cup oil

Filling
1/2 cup provolone, sliced
1/2 lb. salami, sliced
black pepper

1 large bunch parsley, chopped
3 tbsp. olive oil

Bread Dough
Sift flour in large bowl. Mix yeast in warm water until dissolved. Make well in flour, add yeast and salt. Mix and knead for 10 minutes. Pour oil over dough and continue to knead until no longer sticky. Cover dough, let rise until double in bulk.

Divide dough in half. Roll into two rectangular pieces 1/4" thick to fit a cookie sheet with a 1" edge. Combine parsley and oil, spread on dough. Layer provolone and salami on top and sprinkle with pepper. Cover with remaining dough, crimp the edges. Bake in a preheated 350 degree oven for 35-45 minutes until golden brown. Serve warm.

Origin: Aunt Bessie

Margaret Scarfia
John Paul I Lodge #2427

Variation: Escarole Filling
2 heads of escarole, cooked
4 tbsp. olive oil
3 garlic cloves, minced
salt/pepper
1 tbsp. capers

2 tbsp. pine nuts
4 tbsp. raisins
4 anchovy fillets
2 tbsp. pitted black olives
(cut up)

Saute garlic in olive oil, lightly. Add chopped escarole, salt, pepper, pine nuts, raisins, anchovies, black olives and capers. Saute 5 minutes until well blended.

Divide dough in half. Shape each piece like a pizza. Place one circle on an oiled baking sheet. Spread escarole filling to 1" of edge. Place second circle over top. Crimp edges to seal. Bake 25 minutes at 400 degrees.

Renata Curcio Rathmann
La Nuova Sicilia Lodge #1251

Pizza Rustica

Filling

1 lb. dry Italian sausage
  with fennel (slice 1/4")
2 lbs. boiled ham, sliced
1/2 cup Locatelli cheese

1/2 lb. prosciutto, sliced
4 eggs

Crust

4 cups flour
1/4 lb. margarine
4 tbsp. sugar
2 tbsp. parsley, chopped

2 tbsp. baking powder
1/2 cup milk
pinch of salt

Mix crust ingredients, work until smooth. Roll half of dough and place on bottom of pan 11 1/4" x 9 1/4" x 3". Mix cheese, eggs and parsley. Beat well. Pour half into lined pan. Add alternate layers of meat. Cover mix with the rest of the egg mixture. Roll remaining dough over top. Cut several slits on top. Bake at 350 degrees for 45 minutes.

Edith Cuccinelli
Sgt. F.M. Bonanno Lodge #2549

Sciachatta
(Filled Bread)

5 lbs. potatoes, peel & slice
1/2 cup green olives, cracked
1 lb. sweet sausage, remove casing
6 large onions, sliced
4 celery stalks (sliced)
1 large tomato, cut up

1/2 cup capers
1/4 lb. provolone, cut in slices
4 tbsp. olive oil, separated
salt/pepper
olive oil to drizzle
3 lbs. bread dough
  (fresh or frozen)

Filling

Heat two tablespoons of oil in large fry pan. Saute potatoes add a little water and steam to cook (with no color). Put to one side.

Heat 2 tablespoons of oil, add onions, celery and tomato. Saute and steam to cook (with no color). Put to one side.

Saute sausage to cook (with no color). Place potatoes, onions, celery, tomatoes and sausage in a bowl. Add capers and olives.

continued top of next page

Sciachatta

Continued   **(Filled Bread)**

Bread dough
Roll out 2/3 of bread dough (like pizza) to double width of a cookie sheet. Place dough on cookie sheet with one half over-lapped to outside of pan. Fill with 3/4 of the filling. Spread provolone over filling (reserve some cheese for small Sciachatta). Bring over-lapped dough over to cover filling. Crimp the edges and cut slits on top. Drizzle 2 tablespoons of oil in slits. Bake 400 degrees for 20-25 minutes until golden brown. Makes one large and one smaller size. Serves 12 for dinner or 24 appetizer portions.

Edythe Dell'Orfano
Sunrise-Tamarac Lodge #2542

My Mother's Homemade Bread ⭐
(Neopolitan Style)

5 lbs. bread flour	**1 tsp. sugar**
1 pkg. Rapid rise yeast	**7 cups warm water**

Sprinkle yeast and sugar in 4 cups of warm water. Pour 5 lb. bag of flour into a 12-14 quart pot. When yeast bubbles up, add to flour with 3 additional cups of water, mixing in flour with a kneading motion. If a little sticky, add 1/2 cup flour at a time. After completely kneaded into dough, rub entire dough with 1-2 tbsp. olive oil. Set in a warm place to rise, covered for 2 - 2 1/2 hours until doubled in bulk. After dough has risen, place on a floured board. Divide dough into 4 loaves. If dough is sticky, sprinkle flour on hands. Do not handle dough too much. Shape into round loaves. Cover. Let rise until double in size. Bake in a preheated 400 degree oven to a golden brown.

Comment: I have marble slabs cut to fit my electric oven. I place the marble slabs on the grill and preheat the oven. I bake the bread directly on the marble, and it bakes golden brown with a full crispy crust just like an old fashioned stone oven.

As a strapping ten year old boy, I helped my mother knead and bake 50 lbs. of flour twice each week. In those days, we had a thousand acre farm and my father had men from Italy boarding with us, to work the farm. Today, my family enjoys the same bread that I made as a boy. I still bake 5-10 lbs. of flour each week and give it to our children and grandchildren.

John Boniello
Sgt. F.M. Bonanno Lodge #2549

Crescia Marchigiana Style
(Quick Flat Bread)

2 cups flour
1 tsp. baking powder
1 egg, beaten

4 tbsp. shortening
salt
milk to bind (about 1/2 cup)

Blend flour and shortening, baking powder and salt to a crumbly mixture. Add beaten egg and enough milk to bind to a pie dough consistency. Let rest 10 minutes. Cut dough into 4 pieces. Roll out each piece to size of a dinner plate. Prick all over with a fork. Roll out all the dough, placing paper towel between circles of dough.

Prepare frying pan, coat with 3-4 tbsp. olive oil. Heat to fry crescia one at a time. Cook to a light brown, turn with two spatulas, until brown on second side. Layer fried crescia between paper towels. Add olive oil as needed, to fry. Serve with sauteed greens such as swiss chard, spinach, broccoli-rabe, or beet tops and dandelions mixed. Place greens on one half, fold over, and enjoy. Makes four crescia.

Origin: My grandmother, Maria Lorenzini
Born in Tuscany, Italy.

Rose Marie Boniello
Sgt. F. M. Bonanno Lodge #2549

Pepper Biscuits

2 packages dry yeast
2 cups warm water
6 cups flour
4 tsp. fennel seeds
2 tsp. salt

2 tsp. sugar
2 tsp. pepper, coarse grind
1 cup olive oil
1 egg, beaten

Combine yeast, sugar and warm water. Set aside to bubble up and foam. Place flour, fennel seeds, salt and pepper in a large pot. When yeast has foamed, mix gently with olive oil and pour into flour, mixing and turning until dough is formed. Add a little flour if dough is sticky or a little warm water if too stiff. Cover, put in a draft free place for 30 minutes. Roll out into 3" ropes and make pretzel shapes. Brush with beaten egg. Preheat oven to 375 degrees and bake for 30 minutes.

Mary Lozito
Rev. Albert Palombo Lodge #2512

Zeppole ⭐
(Flour and Potato Dough)

10 cups flour
3 eggs, beaten
1 tsp. salt
3 packages dry yeast
1/2 cup margarine
1 1/2 cups warm potato water

3 potatoes, peeled
　(boiled and mashed)
3 tbsp. sugar
1/2 cup shortening
1 cup milk
oil for frying

In a large bowl, mix warm water from potatoes, milk, margarine, shortening, yeast, sugar, salt and mashed potatoes. Cover and set aside.

Make a well in center of flour, add eggs and liquid ingredients and mix with wooden spoon. Dough will be soft and elastic. If necessary add a little more flour. Beat well, cover bowl and let rise for 1 hour, punch dough down and let rise an additional hour.

To make zeppole: Oil hands, take a piece of dough the size of a large walnut, stretch and twist then fry in hot oil. When cool, sprinkle zeppole with confectioners sugar or dip them in warm honey.

Origin: Great Uncle Carmen Battigliera

Valerie and Ray Laurie
Sgt. F. M. Bonanno Lodge #2549

Zeppole ⭐
(Fried Dough)

4 cups flour
1/2 tsp. salt
oil for frying

1 pkg, dry yeast
2 cups warm water
confectioners sugar

Dissolve yeast in warm water. Mix flour and salt in a bowl; add yeast and additional warm water, as needed. Work dough until sticky and loose. Let rise until double in bulk.

Oil hands, pull about a tablespoonful of dough and stretch until about 3-4" long. Gently drop into hot oil and fry until golden brown. When cool, sprinkle with confectioners sugar.

When Mom makes "zeppole", we are all standing around the stove waiting for them to brown. We eat them as fast as she makes them and hardly leave any for her.

Origin: My mom, Josephine Miele

Lucy Yonnetti
Sgt. F. M. Bonanno Lodge #2549

Zeppole
(Christmas Fried Dough)

8 cups flour
1 pkg. dry yeast
salt/pepper
warm water, as needed

1 cup raisins
1 cup pignoli nuts
2 oz. anchovy fillets, optional
oil for frying

Soften yeast in one cup of warm water. When yeast has dissolved and is foamy, add to flour, salt and pepper. Add warm water to make a smooth elastic, almost runny dough. Work the dough through your fingers for about 5 minutes to blend all the flour. Set in a warm place to rise. When dough has doubled, work the dough down to rise a second time.

Heat oil; the oil is ready when a cube of bread pops to the surface and is lightly browned. Oil your fingers and sprinkle just a few raisins and pine nuts over the dough. Pull a piece of dough the size of a golf ball and lightly work in 3-4 raisins and nuts. Roll the dough around your fingers, shaping a ball. Drop gently into the hot oil and fry until golden brown. Continue to sprinkle just a few raisins and nuts over the dough as you fry each batch of zeppoles. May also add 2-3 pieces of anchovy fillets to raisins and nuts, as you fry.

Zeppole are traditional to our family, served at noon Christmas Eve Day with Zuppa di Baccala and with honey on our Christmas Eve buffet table.

Origin: *Grandma Rosina Boniello, San Nazzaro, Italy*

Rose Marie Boniello
Sgt. F. M. Bonanno Lodge #2549

Brignolata
(Sausage Roll)

1 lb. bread dough
2 tbsp. red wine
1 egg, beaten

1 lb. Italian sausage
(remove casing)

Add wine to sausage, mix well and divide in 4 equal parts. Divide dough into 4 parts, roll each piece 1/4" thick, 3" wide and 12" long. Spread sausage along the length of the dough, fold and seal edges. Roll each strip around your finger to form a pinwheel. Tuck the ends under. Brush top with beaten egg and bake in a preheated oven 350 degrees for 35-40 minutes until brown. Serve warm. *Served at Christmas and festive occasions.*

Grace Campisi
La Nuova Sicilia Lodge #1251

Panettone di Pasqua ✯
(Easter Bread)

1 pkg. yeast	6 eggs, beaten
3/4 cup butter, melted	5-6 cups flour
1/4 tsp. salt	2/3 cups seedless raisins
1 cup sugar	1/2 cup candied citron, diced

Soften yeast in 1/4 cup warm water. Combine cooled butter, salt, sugar and eggs blending well. Add 3 1/2 cups of flour beating to a smooth consistency. Add yeast and remaining flour to form a soft bread dough. Let rise in a warm place until double in bulk. Punch dough down twice. On second rise, blend raisins and citron evenly. Shape in a ring. Place on a greased cookie sheet, cover and let rise until double in size. Bake 375 degrees for 10 minutes, then lower heat to 325 degrees. Bake an additional 35-40 minutes until golden brown. While still warm frost with confectioners sugar icing, sprinkle with colored sprinkles. Makes a very large bread.

Note: Dough can be separated in half after the second rise to make 1 small ring, then bake the remaining dough in a greased 1 lb. coffee can. Let rise to double bulk before baking. Bake both at 375 degrees for 10 minutes then 25-30 minutes at 325 degrees until golden brown, frost with confectioners sugar icing while still warm.

Icing: 1/2 cup confectioners sugar mixed with enough water to make a soft smooth icing.

Thru the years when the entire family was seated for Easter dinner, grandma Boniello would bring the Panettone to the table and place it in front of grandpa to cut the first slice. She would then say a little prayer and ask God to bless grandpa and the family. We would then say Grace and start our meal.

Our family continues this tradition and bless the men in our family each year at the start of our Easter dinner.

Origin: Grandma Rosina Boniello

**Rose Marie Boniello
Sgt. F. M. Bonanno Lodge #2549**

Pizza Rustica

Dough

2 1/4 cups flour	4 tbsp. lard
1/2 tsp. salt	water

Cut lard and salt into flour, add water to form dough, knead. Cut in half and roll as pie crust to line bottom and sides of a 3 quart pyrex dish. Roll remaining dough to cover filling.

Filling

3 lbs. ricotta	1 chicken breast, diced
1/2 tsp. pepper	1/2 lb. basket cheese, diced
1/4 cup Parmesan cheese	2 hard boiled eggs, diced
1 Abruzzese sausage, diced	1/4 lb. prosciuto, sliced thin
6 oz. pepperoni, diced	6 eggs, beaten

Mix all ingredients together, except prosciuto. Pour 1/2 of the mixture in the lined baking dish, then layer slices of prosciuto over top. Pour in balance of the mixture and top with prosciuto. Place dough over top and crimp edges. Brush with a beaten egg white. Bake 350 degrees for 2 hours or until knife set in center comes out clean.

Easter tradition, Abruzzi, Italy

M. Palma Guarente
Coral Springs Lodge #2332

Variation

1/4 lb. salami	1 lb. dry sausage
1/2 lb. prosciuto	1/4 lb. basket cheese
1 tbsp. Parmesan cheese	8-10 eggs, beaten

Cut all ingredients into cubes. Add to eggs and parmesan cheese. Mix well and pour into a round pan that has been lined with dough. Cover filling with dough or lattice strips. Bake 350 degrees for 1 hour and 15 minutes. Test with knife if center is dry.

Easter tradition, Naples, Italy

Vito J. Rossi
Charles J. Bonaparte Lodge #2504

Pizza Ripieno/Pizza Rustica

Dough
2 cups flour
2 eggs
1/4 cup oil

1/3 cup water
1/4 tsp. black pepper

Beat eggs into oil and water. Blend into flour and pepper and form a pie crust dough. Knead for a few minutes and let rest covered.

Filling
8 eggs, beaten
1/2 tsp. coarse ground pepper
1 lb. ricotta
1 cup Parmesan cheese

10-12 slices prosciuto
10-12 slices salami
1 lb. basket cheese, sliced

Combine eggs, pepper, ricotta and grated cheese. Blend well.

Divide dough in half. Roll each piece into a circle to line a 9" deep pie pan. Pour 1/2 ricotta mixture into pan, layer proscuito and salami over top. Cover with remaining ricotta. Layer top with fresh basket cheese slices. Cover with dough, crimp edges and seal. Bake in preheated oven 350 degrees, 1 hour 10 minutes.

Origin: Easter tradition in my family from Bari, Italy.

Jeanette D'Alessandro
Coral Springs Lodge #2332

Variation: Omit basket cheese, and add 1/2 lb. provolone, cubed.

Origin: Easter tradition in Avellino, Italy.

Ellen C. Feigenbaum
Ft. Lauderdale Lodge #2263

Pizza "Pien" Ripieno

Dough

10 cups bread flour
1 pkg. rapid-rise yeast
1 egg, beaten
2 tbsp. lard, melted

1/4 cup Parmesan cheese
2 tsp. coarse ground pepper
3 1/2 cups warm water

Soften yeast in 1/2 cup warm water. Blend together egg, lard, pepper, cheese and 3 cups warm water. Add yeast. Add 3 cups of flour and beat thoroughly. Add remaining flour gradually and mix to form dough. Knead 8-10 minutes. Cover and let rise until double in bulk.

Filling

1 lb. piece prosciutto, diced
6 oz. pepperoni, diced
1 lb. fresh basket cheese, sliced

3 1/2 cups Parmesan cheese
16 eggs, beaten
1 1/2 lbs. ricotta

Combine parmesan cheese, eggs and ricotta. Add prosciutto and pepperoni. Divide into 4 portions.

Punch down the dough. Divide into 8 portions. Roll 2 pieces to fit a deep 10" pyrex pie plate. Pour in 1/4 of the filling, layer 1/4 of the cheese slices over top. Cover with rolled dough. Fold edge onto the pizza to make a tight seal. Recipe makes 4 pizza "Pien". Make a small slit in the center. Let pizza rise 15 minutes. Bake 350 degree oven for 1 hour until golden brown. (We serve the pizza at 12:00 noon Holy Saturday.)

Grandma Rosina Boniello always raised extra dough then shaped and baked a "Gingerbread Man" with his arms wrapped around an egg for each of the grandchildren. We continue this Easter tradition in our family.

Origin: My mother-in-law Rose Marie Boniello

Christine Boniello
Submitted by John Boniello
Sgt. F. M. Bonanno Lodge #2549

Easter Bread Ring ☆

5 uncooked eggs, colored
2 pkgs. dry yeast
3/4 cup shortening
3 eggs
1 cup sugar
colored sprinkles

1 cup warm water
6 cups flour
2 tbsp. lemon juice
1 tbsp. lemon rind, grated
food dye to color eggs

Yeast sponge: Soften yeast in warm water. Blend in 1 1/2 cups of flour and mix well. Cover with wax paper and a towel, set in warm place to rise for 1 1/2-2 hours.

Cream the shortening, sugar and 2 eggs plus 1 egg white until thick. Add lemon juice and rind. Blend the egg mixture into the yeast sponge, together with 4 1/2 cups of flour to form a soft dough. Add additional flour as needed. Place in a greased bowl, cover and let rise until double in bulk, about 1 1/2-2 hours.

Punch down, divide dough in half. Roll each piece into a rope forming a loose braid. Space 5 eggs into the loops of the braided ring. Cover, let rise until doubled. Bake 350 degrees for 10 minutes. Then brush with 1 egg yolk mixed with 1 tbsp. milk. Bake an additional 40-45 minutes.

Adeline Villana-McNulty
Sons of Italy Lodge #321
Schenectedy, NY

Vuccidrato ☆
(St. Joseph Bread)

1 cup sugar
2 tsp. salt
3 eggs
1 qt. warm water

2 pkgs. dry yeast
1/2 cup corn oil
16 cups bread flour
1 egg, beaten

In a bowl mix sugar, salt, eggs, water, yeast and oil. Then mix in the flour. Knead dough on a floured board until smooth. Let rise.

Cut the dough in thirds. Shape each piece into a rope then twist like a braid. Bring the ends together and tuck in both ends to form a ring. Make a shallow cut 1 1/2" apart around the outside of the ring. Place on a greased baking sheet. Let rise until double in bulk. Bake in a hot 400 degree oven for 30-40 minutes until golden brown.

Carmela Cannata
Unita Lodge #2015

Crescia
(Easter Cheese Bread)

1 pkg. dry yeast
1/2 cup warm water
5 eggs, beaten
1/2 cup warm milk
1 pkg. sharp cracker barrel cheese
  (cut into 1/2" cubes)

1/2 cup butter, melted
2 cups Parmesan cheese
6-6 1/2 cups flour
1 tbsp. coarse ground pepper

Dissolve yeast in warm water until foam has formed. Mix eggs, milk, butter and parmesan cheese. Add yeast, stir to blend in, then add flour slowly to form a soft bread dough. Knead for about 5 minutes. Let rise until double in size. Turn dough out onto a lightly floured board and roll to about 1/2" thickness. Spread cubed cheese over top then roll as a jelly roll, tuck ends in. Place into a greased tall tube pan and let rise until double in size. Bake in a preheated 350 degree oven for 40-45 minutes until golden in color.

My grandmother brought this recipe from Senigalia, Italy as a young bride. My mother carried the tradition and I have passed it along to my daughters and daughter-in-law.

Origin: *My mother, Elena Giuliani*

Rose Marie Boniello
Sgt. F. M. Bonanno Lodge #2549

Herb Bread Roll

1/4 lb. black olives, chopped
1/4 lb. green olives, chopped
2 oz. can anchovies, mashed
1 tbsp. capers
1/2 cup cooked mushrooms
  (chopped)
1/3 cup Olive oil

2 tbsp. parsley, chopped
2 garlic cloves, chopped
4-5 fresh basil leaves
  (chopped)
1/2 tsp. hot pepper flakes
1 lb. bread dough
  (fresh or frozen)

Roll out bread dough to about 1/2" thickness in a rectangular shape. Mix all ingredients and spread on top of the dough to 1" of the edges. Roll up dough in a jelly roll form. Pinch edges and lay on the seam.
Bake in a preheated oven 400 degrees about 30 minutes until golden brown. Let cool slightly then slice.

Jennie Caltagirone
La Nuova Sicilia Lodge #1251

LE UOVA/
EGGS

Pomodoro con Uove di Mondolfo
(Stewed Tomatoes and Eggs Mondolfo Style)

1 medium onion, sliced	3 tbsp. olive oil
1/2 can peeled tomatoes, crushed	4 eggs
chopped parsley	salt/pepper

In a small fry pan, saute onion in olive oil with salt and pepper until wilted and soft. Add tomatoes, parsley, cook until oil separates about 10-15 minutes. Stirring often. As tomatoes simmer, gently break 4 eggs (spaced) and let poach until yolks are cooked to your liking. Lots of crusty bread to soak up the tomato and a salad makes a great lunch for two.

My father enjoyed this dish with a piece of cheese, black olives and a glass (or two) of his homemade wine. As a child, I remember he would cook this lunch just for the two of us and pour me a little wine (when my mother was out).

Rose Marie Boniello
Sgt. F. M. Bonanno Lodge #2549

Pasta Frittata

1/2 lb. thin spaghetti, cooked	1/3 cup chopped Fontina cheese
1/3 cup Parmesan cheese	1/2 lb. spinach, blanched
2 tbsp. Italian parsley, chopped	3 eggs, slightly beaten
1 tbsp. olive oil	salt/pepper

Mix together all ingredients except oil. Heat a large, non-stick skillet (about 10"), add oil, and when it is medium-hot, add the mixture, spreading it evenly in the skillet. Cook over medium heat for about 5 minutes, or until bottom of frittata has formed a golden crust. Invert frittata onto a plate , then slip it back into the skillet to brown the other side. Cook until a crust is formed.

Cut into wedges and serve, with more cheese, if desired.

Note: This is a delicious way to use up leftover pasta. The variety of ingredients you may include in a pasta frittata are chopped fresh tomatoes, leftover vegetables or meat, a mix of herbs, or mozzarella cheese, to name a few.

Rose Malzone
Ft. Lauderdale Lodge #2263

Broccoli Frittata

2 1/2 tbsp. onion, chopped
1 pkg. frozen chopped broccoli
   (cooked and drained)
2 1/2 tbsp. Parmesan cheese
1/4 cup milk
1/2 cup mozzarella cheese,
   shredded

2 tbsp. butter or margarine
1 small garlic clove, crushed
1 cup Rice, cooked
2 eggs, slightly beaten
1/2 tsp. salt
dash of pepper

Saute onion in butter until tender. Do not brown. Add broccoli, garlic, rice and parmesan cheese, mix well. Combine eggs, milk and seasonings. Stir into rice mixture. Turn into well-buttered shallow 1 qt. casserole. Top with mozzarella cheese. Bake at 350 degrees for 20-25 minutes until set. Makes 2 servings.

Ellen C. Feigenbaum
Ft. Lauderdale Lodge #2263

Zucchini Frittata

6 large eggs
4 tbsp. butter or margarine
1 med. onion, thinly sliced
2 tbsp. chopped parsley
salt\pepper

1/3 cup Parmesan cheese
1 tbsp. olive oil
3 zucchini, thinly sliced
2 garlic cloves, chopped

Beat eggs, salt, pepper in medium bowl. Melt 2 tbsp. butter with oil in heavy skillet, when butter foams add onions, saute over medium heat. Add zucchini, parsley and garlic until lightly browned. Remove zucchini with slotted spoon, stir into egg mixture. Melt remaining butter in skillet, when butter foams, add egg mixture, cook over medium heat 5-6 minutes until bottom of frittata is brown. Place large plate on top of frittata and turn over. Cook 5-6 minutes on other side. Serve hot.

Mary Dalfonzo
Sgt. F. M. Bonanno Lodge #2549

Pepperoni Frittata

1 cup onions, chopped
1 cup cooked cauliflower
  (or any cooked vegetable)
5 eggs, slightly beaten
4 or 5 oz. pepperoni, sliced

1 Zucchini
  (thinly sliced)
2-3 tbsp. olive oil
1/3 cup parmesan cheese

In medium skillet saute onion and zucchini in oil until tender. Add cauliflower. In a bowl stir eggs, cheese and pepperoni until blended. Pour over vegetables in skillet. Cook over low heat about 15 minutes until set. If surface is moist, run skillet under broiler one minute or less to set the surface. Serve from skillet or slide onto serving plate. Cut into pie shaped wedges to serve.

BUON APPETITO!

Laura Spoto
La Nuova Sicilia Lodge #1251

Burdock (Cardoon) Frittata

2-3 eggs, beaten
1 tsp. parsley
salt\pepper

2 tbsp. Romano cheese
1 bunch cardoon
1 garlic clove

Clean and wash cardoon thoroughly, cut into 2" pieces. Boil until tender, drain well.

Put olive oil in fry pan, add 1 clove garlic saute a few minutes, remove garlic. Add cardoon and saute about 10 minutes. Mix eggs, parsley and cheese. Pour mixture over cardoon. Fry as an omelet, then flip, using a round dinner plate, to brown on other side. Cut in wedges. Good between 2 slices of crusty Italian bread.

Mary Sorci
John Paul I Lodge #2427

Pisci d'Ovu Con Fagioli Fresce e Macaroni
(Egg Fritters with String Beans and Macaroni)

1 lb. string beans, cut in pieces
   (boiled until tender)
1/2 lb. macaroni, ziti, etc.
3/4 cup bread crumbs
   (unflavored)
1/2 tsp. garlic, chopped fine
chopped parsley

Marinara Sauce
6 tbsp. grated Parmesan cheese
6 eggs, beaten
salt\pepper
oil to fry
(1" in small skillet)

Egg Fritters:

Add bread crumbs, cheese, parsley, salt, pepper and garlic to eggs. Mix thoroughly to form a batter. Heat oil to medium high, when hot, a drop of batter should stiffen and float to the surface. Put in batter a teaspoonful at a time. Do not crowd. When fritters have puffed up, turn them until they form a golden crust.

Combine string beans, macaroni and marinara sauce in a large serving bowl. Add egg fritters and toss gently. Serve at once. Serves 4.

Josephine Ragone
Jerry Barletta Lodge #2502

Asparagus Frittata

8 eggs, beaten well
1 large onion, sliced thin
3 oz. grated Romano cheese
salt\pepper

1/2 lb. asparagus, 2" lengths
1/4 cup olive oil
6 oz. mozzarella, shredded

Saute onion and asparagus in oil 10-12 minutes or until onions are golden. Be careful not to brown. Mix grated cheese with eggs and pour eggs over vegetables. Move egg mixture from edge of pan allowing oil to seep through eggs. When eggs are 3/4 cooked, slide frittata out of pan onto dish. Invert pan over dish, add mozzarella on top, place under broiler for a minute. Slide omelet onto serving platter. Garnish with slices of tomato and parsley.

Frank W. Ricci
Justin Antonin Scalia Lodge #2235

PRIMI PIATTI - SALSE/ FIRST COURSES - SAUCE

Calamari Sauce

2 lbs. whole squid w/tentacles
4 tbsp. olive oil
2 garlic cloves, chopped
pinch of oregano
salt/pepper

1 large can plum tomatoes
(crushed or pureed in blender)
1 tbsp. parsley, chopped
1/2 cup dry sherry

Add tomatoes to saucepan with parsley, oregano, salt and pepper. Simmer for 30 minutes.

In a frying pan, add olive oil and lightly brown garlic cloves. Add cut up squid and saute for about 10 minutes. Add 1/2 cup dry sherry, stir; pour into tomato sauce and simmer gently for about 15 minutes. Serve over your favorite pasta.

To Prepare Squid for Cooking:
Separate tentacles from sac, squeeze out boney beak. Wash sac thoroughly, removing thin translucent bone. Peel off any outer skin. Cut sac into rings. Tentacles may be left whole or cut in half.

Origin: "Grandma Beece"

Victoria Casario
Jerry Barletta Lodge #2502

Variation
Omit parsley, oregano and dry sherry.

Substitute
2 tbsp. fresh mint leaves, chopped   1 bottle clam juice
4 garlic cloves, chopped

Saute garlic in olive oil with salt and pepper just until garlic turns pale in color. Add tomatoes, simmer 20 minutes. Add mint leaves and squid. Simmer gently 15 minutes until squid is tender.

Origin: Grandma Maria Lorenzini, Tuscany

Rose Marie Boniello
Sgt. F. M. Bonanno Lodge #2549

Shrimp Sauce

1 lb. fresh shrimp
2 small onions, chopped
1/4 tsp. salt and pepper
1/4 cup oil
1/4 cup Romano cheese, optional

2 garlic cloves, minced
1 green pepper, chopped
1/8 tsp. oregano
1 lb. Spaghetti

Boil shrimp until barely tender. Shell and devein. Saute garlic, onions, green pepper, salt, pepper and oregano in oil until onions are soft. Add cooked shrimp. Stir and cook over low heat for 10 minutes. Cook spaghetti until al dente, drain and toss gently with shrimp mixture. Sprinkle with cheese.

Buono Appetito "Ya'll"

Ann Varalla
Joseph A. Franzalia Lodge #2422

Clam Sauce

2 doz. fresh topneck clams or
   (2 small cans chopped clams)
1/4 cup olive oil
1 4 oz. bottle clam juice

1/4 cup parsley, chopped
6 garlic cloves, chopped
1/4 cup grated cheese, optional
1 lb. linguine

To open fresh clams:
Rinse in cold water, place in plastic bag and put in freezer for 2 hours. Remove clams from shells, reserving clam juice. Coarsely chop clams.

Saute garlic in olive oil until golden in color. Add juice from clams and bottled clam juice. Boil gently for 2 minutes. Add clams and simmer 2-4 minutes until clams are tender. Add parsley, pour clam sauce over linguine. Serves 4-5.

Vincent Lupo
Justin Antonin Scalia Lodge #2235

Tuna Sauce

2 tbsp. olive oil
1 garlic clove, crushed
1 small can plum tomatoes
pepper

1/2 medium onion, chopped
3 anchovy fillets
1 (6 1/2) oz. can tuna
1/2 lb. penne

Heat oil in a frying pan, add onions and saute 5 minutes. Add garlic, cook until onions start to brown. Add anchovies. Crush them with a spoon. Add tomatoes, simmer covered to form a sauce about 15 minutes. Drain the tuna and break into large flakes; add tuna to sauce with a little pepper (anchovies and tuna are already salty). Simmer, uncovered, for 5 minutes. Juices will evaporate and sauce will thicken. Serves 2.

Rose Malzone
Ft. Lauderdale Lodge #2263

Tuna Fish Sauce with Bow Ties

4 tbsp. olive oil
2 garlic cloves, crushed
3 anchovy fillets
1 can tuna with oil

8 fresh plum tomatoes, chopped
2 tbsp. mint leaves, chopped
1/2 lb. bow ties, pasta
salt/pepper

Saute garlic, salt and pepper to a pale color. Add anchovies, crush with a wooden spoon. Add tuna with oil. Break into flakes, stir and saute 2-3 minutes. Add tomatoes and mint leaves. Simmer for 15 minutes covered. Uncover and simmer 5 minutes longer. Serve over bow ties cooked al dente.

Origin: Family favorite

Rose Marie Boniello
Sgt. F. M. Bonanno Lodge #2549

Salsa per Pesce
(Sauce for Grilled Fish)

2 eggs, hard boiled
2/3 cup olive oil

4 anchovy fillets
6-7 drops lemon juice

Chop egg yolks and anchovy fillets separately. Combine them in a mortar and pestle. Blend until smooth. Gradually stir in oil and lemon juice until sauce has a creamy consistency. Serve over grilled or broiled fish.

Anthony Simione
John Paul I Lodge #2427

Salsa per Pesce al Forno
(Baked Fish Sauce)

1/4 cup olive oil
2 garlic cloves, minced
hot pepper flakes, optional
1 tsp. fresh ground black pepper
1 tbsp. cold water
2 stalks fennel or celery, minced
1/2 cup dry red wine
2 tbsp. Italian parsley, minced
4 tbsp. capers, drained

2 large onions, minced
3 whole cloves
2 tsp. salt
1 tbsp. all purpose flour
3 cups peeled, chopped tomatoes
   (fresh or canned)
1 cup green olives
   (sliced/pitted)
3 lbs. firm thick fish
   (snapper, cod, shark, halibut)

Preheat oven 350 degrees.

Rinse fish and pat dry on paper towel. Arrange one layer in greased baking dish. Heat oil in a skillet, add onion and garlic cook for 1 minute, stirring to prevent browning, add tomatoes, fennel, wine, cloves, hot pepper flakes, salt and pepper. Cover and simmer on low heat for about 20 minutes. Mix flour and water to a smooth paste. Pour flour paste into sauce, stirring constantly for smooth mixture. Continue cooking and stirring for 5 minutes. Mix in parsley, olives and capers. Pour over fish and bake uncovered for 30 minutes, baste occasionally until fish flakes easily with fork. Serve with your favorite pasta or rice.

Lena McKendree
Unita Lodge #2015

Sword Fish Sauce

2 lbs. sword fish steaks
2 stalks of celery with leaves
   (chopped)
2 tbsp. capers

2 cans (28 oz.) Italian plum
   tomatoes (pureed)
1 onion, chopped
1 lb. linguine, cooked al dente

Saute celery, onion and capers until soft, add pureed tomatoes - cook 1/2 hour. Add sword fish and simmer slowly until fish flakes about 15 minutes.

To serve: Remove fish to a serving platter. Reserve a little pasta water and add to sauce, if needed.

Josephine Miracola
Ft. Lauderdale Lodge #2263

Onion Sauce with Eye Round Roast Beef

3 lbs. onions, diced
4-6 lbs. eye round roast
2 cans Italian plum tomatoes
1/4 cup fresh basil, chopped
1 tsp. salt
2 lbs. Large Bow Ties, macaroni

3-4 tbsp. olive oil or
  (4 tbsp. salt pork, diced)
1 can tomato paste
2 garlic cloves
1/2 tsp. pepper

Saute diced onions about 20 minutes in olive oil stirring every few minutes. Add tomato paste and cook for 2-3 minutes. Put plum tomatoes in blender for a few seconds, just to blend, add tomatoes and garlic to pot with onions and paste.

In separate pan, brown eye round on all sides in a small amount of oil. Add meat to sauce and simmer slowly for 3 hrs. Remove garlic cloves. Recommended macaroni for this sauce is large egg bowties. Carve roast into thin slices and serve with extra sauce. The large quantity of onions make this a sweet, delicious sauce. Serves 8-10.

Andrew Verdirame
Submitted by Gladys Marino
Sunrise-Tamarac Lodge #2452

Prosciutto and Onion Sauce alla Verdirame

3-4 large onions, diced
3 garlic cloves, minced
  (or 1/2 tsp. garlic powder)
2 large cans Italian plum tomatoes
  (puree in blender)
1/4 tsp. black and white pepper

3 tbsp. olive oil
1/4 lb. prosciutto, diced
1 small can tomato sauce (8 oz.)
1/2 cup fresh basil, chopped
  (1 tbsp. dried basil)
1/4 tsp. salt

Saute onions with garlic in olive oil for about 5 minutes. Add prosciutto and cook a few minutes longer. Add tomato sauce and simmer for about 3-4 minutes. Add plum tomatoes, salt, pepper and cook 1 hour. Serve over linguine or your favorite macaroni.

Andrew Verdirame
Submitted by Gladys Marino
Sunrise-Tamarac Lodge #2452

Sun Dried Tomato Sauce

1/4 lb. butter
1 large onion, chopped
3 tbsp. fresh parsley, chopped
4 oz. Sundried tomatoes, cut up
1/2 pt. half and half
4 tbsp. red wine
1 lb. Rigatoni or Ziti Rigati

1/2 cup olive oil
6-8 garlic cloves, chopped
3 tbsp. fresh basil, chopped
1 1/2 pt. heavy cream
1 small can tomato paste
freshly ground black pepper

Soak Sundried tomatoes in hot water for 30 minutes, drain.

In large frying pan, melt butter with olive oil, add chopped onion and cook until softened. Add garlic, stir until garlic starts to color, add basil and parsley stir a few more minutes then add Sundried tomatoes. Simmer a few minutes (do not overcook), add heavy cream and half and half. Cook over low heat until blended, do not boil. Add tomato paste, heat until smooth and blended, add pepper to taste and toss immediately with al dente pasta. Pass freshly grated cheese and fresh ground pepper.

Marie Vitelli
New Brunswick, N.J.
Submitted by Ann Borgia
Sgt. F. M. Bonanno Lodge #2549

Salsa di Pomodoro e Carne Macinata ☆
(Quick Tomato Sauce with Ground Beef)

2 tbsp. olive oil
1/2 medium onion, chopped
1 large can plum tomatoes
   (chopped in blender)
6 oz. can tomato paste
   (diluted with 6 oz. water)

1 garlic clove, chopped
1 lb. ground beef
1-2 fresh basil leaves
   (1/2 tsp. dry)
salt/pepper

Heat olive oil in saucepan and lightly saute garlic and onion. Add ground beef, stirring until browned. Slowly stir in tomatoes, tomato paste, water, basil, salt and pepper. Cover and simmer 45 minutes stirring occasionally.

Louise Vallone
Sgt. F. M. Bonanno Lodge #2549

Meat Sauce for Polenta/Pasta ✯
(Italian Sausage and Chuck Steak)

1 large onion, chopped
2 garlic cloves, minced
3 tbsp. olive oil
2 lbs. lean boneless chuck steak
   (cubed)
salt/pepper

1 lb. sweet sausage
2 tsp. oregano
2 tsp. crushed red pepper
   (optional)
2 large cans tomato puree

In a large pot, saute onion and garlic in olive oil until soft. Gradually add chuck steak and sausage and cook until well browned. Stir in tomatoes, add oregano, salt, pepper and red pepper. Bring to a boil and cover, lower heat and simmer until meat is tender. If sauce is too thick add a little hot water. Serves 6-8

Vinnie Fragala
Township Sons of Italy Lodge #2624

Carbonara Sauce

6 slices bacon, diced
1/2 cup heavy cream
2 egg yolks, plus 1 yolk
1 lb. Spaghetti

1/4 cup butter
salt/pepper
1/3 cup Parmesan cheese

Saute bacon in butter, remove with a slotted spoon. Keep hot. Beat eggs in a large bowl with cream and pepper. Pour into a bowl with hot cooked spaghetti, toss to mix well. Sprinkle with bacon and parmesan cheese.

Variation: 1 cup slivered ham
1/4 tsp. red pepper flakes

Origin: Mamma Carolina

Nancy Tarantino
Jerry Barletta Lodge #2502

Salsa di Carne al Pomodoro
(Tomato Meat Sauce)

1/4 cup olive oil	3 garlic cloves, chopped
1 medium onion, chopped	2 large cans plum tomatoes
6 oz. can tomato paste	(chopped in blender)
(dilute with 8 oz. water)	3 fresh basil leaves
1 tsp. salt	1 bay leaf
1/4 tsp. pepper	1 lb. Italian sausage
1/2 lb. port shoulder or loin end	1/2 lb. beef chuck

Lightly brown meat in skillet with olive oil, salt and pepper. Set aside.

In a saucepan, heat olive oil, garlic and onion, brown lightly. Add blended tomatoes, salt, pepper, basil and bay leaf. Cover and simmer for 1/2 hour. Add tomato paste (diluted) and when it comes to a boil add all meats. Simmer covered for 1 1/2 hours. Remove meat and bay leaf from sauce. Serve over pasta with Parmesan or Romano cheese.

Meatballs

1 lb. ground beef	2 eggs
1 garlic clove, chopped	2 tbsp. parsley, chopped
1/2 cup bread crumbs	3 tbsp. grated Italian cheese
salt/pepper	

Mix all ingredients in a bowl and form into approximately 1 1/2" round balls. In a skillet with 2 tbsp. olive oil, lightly brown meat balls on all side. Add to sauce and simmer 15 - 20 minutes.

Louise Vallone
Sgt. F. M. Bonanno Lodge #2549

Herb Sauce

1/4 lb. black olives, chopped	2 tbsp. parsley, chopped
1/4 lb. green olives, chopped	2 garlic cloves, chopped
2 oz. can anchovies, mashed	4-5 large basil leaves
1 tbsp. capers	(chopped)
1/2 cup precooked mushrooms	1/2 tsp. hot pepper flakes
(chopped)	1/3 cup olive oil
1 lb. spaghetti, çooked	

Mix all ingredients together, put on low heat to warm up slowly. Stir and keep hot. Pour over hot spaghetti, mix gently to serve. NO GRATED CHEESE.

Jennie Caltagirone
La Nuova Sicilia Lodge #1251

Basic Marinara Sauce

3-4 tbsp. olive oil
1 16 oz. can crushed tomatoes
1/4 tsp. oregano

1 garlic clove, minced
1 tsp. dried basil
salt/pepper

Lightly saute garlic in olive oil. Remove pan from heat. Add crushed tomatoes, basil, oregano, salt and pepper, return to medium heat. Simmer for 30 minutes, adding a little water as needed, so as not to stick. Sauce for 1 lb. of pasta.

Lucy Yonnetti
Sgt. F. M. Bonanno Lodge #2549

Variation
Replace basil and oregano with 3-4 tbsp. chopped parsley. Add hot pepper flakes along with salt and pepper to crushed tomatoes, then simmer.

Ginette M. Reish
Joseph A. Franzalia Lodge #2422

Variation
1 small onion, chopped
2 garlic cloves, minced
1/4 cup olive oil
1 (28 oz.) Plum tomatoes, crushed
salt/pepper

1/4 cup dry white wine
1 tbsp. fresh parsley, chopped
1 tbsp. fresh basil, chopped
1/4 tsp. fennel seed
(may be powdered in blender)

Following instructions for Basic Marinara Sauce, saute onion and garlic together in olive oil, add wine to tomatoes along with spices.

Virginia Minghella
Mike Accardi Lodge #2441

Fettuccine all' Alfredo
(Alfredo Sauce)

1 cup heavy cream
2 cups parmesan cheese
pepper, freshly ground

1 stick of butter, softened
pinch of nutmeg
1 lb. Fettuccine, cooked al dente

In a cook and serve enameled cast-iron pan, place 2/3 cup of cream and all the butter. Simmer over low heat for about 1 minute until butter and cream have thickened slightly. Remove from heat, add drained Fettuccine to pan and return to stove on low heat. Toss Fettuccine, coating with sauce. Add rest of cream, grated cheese, salt and nutmeg. Toss briefly until sauce has thickened. Serve immediately with fresh ground pepper.

Antoinette Zaffarano
Sgt. F. M. Bonanno Lodge #2549

Salsa di Caserta
(Cream Sauce with Sweet Sausage, Green Peppers)

1 1/2 lb. sweet sausage
1 cup onion, chopped
1 garlic clove, minced
1/4 cup parsley, minced
1/2 tsp. salt
1/2 cup Parmesan cheese

1 large green pepper,
  (chopped coarsely)
1 cup light cream
1 tsp. dried marjoram, crushed
1/8 tsp. pepper
1 lb. rotelli pasta, al dente

Remove sausage from casing, crumble into a skillet. Stir and cook until sausage is no longer pink. Add onion and garlic, saute until onion is soft and light colored. Drain excess fat. Stir in cream, parsley, cheese, marjoram, salt and pepper. Bring to a low simmer (do not boil), reduce heat, cook and stir over medium heat 6-8 minutes until thickened.

Serve over pasta.

Origin: Caserta, Italy

Marie Lotito
Rev. Albert B. Palombo Lodge #2512

Silvana's Sausage and Eggplant Sauce

1 lb. Italian sweet sausage
1 eggplant
2 large garlic cloves, mashed
10 fresh parsley sprigs, leaves only
3 tbsp. olive oil
1/4 cup butter
Spaghetti

1/4 lb. onions, diced
1 tsp. salt
1/4 tsp. pepper
3 green peppers, sliced thin
3 cups peeled canned tomatoes
  (chopped)
Parmesan cheese

Remove sausage from casing, crumble into small pieces. Wash and dry eggplant do not peel. Cut into 6 crosswise slices and then into 1/2" cubes. Chop garlic and parsley together.

Combine oil and butter in saucepan and heat. Add onions and cook until medium brown. Add sausage, brown for 10 minutes. Add garlic, parsley, salt, pepper and cook for 10 minutes longer. Add green peppers, eggplant cubes and tomatoes. Stir and cook for 45 minutes, slowly. Serve sauce over cooked spaghetti and pass the Parmesan cheese.

Silvana R. Graham
La Nuova Sicilia Lodge #1251

Pesto Sauce

1 cup fresh basil leaves, packed
4 garlic cloves
1/4 cup grated Italian cheese
salt/pepper

1 cup fresh parsley, packed
1/4 cup pignoli nuts
1 cup olive oil

Place all ingredients in a blender, blend together using low speed with 1/2 cup of olive oil. Stop every few seconds to scrape the sides of the blender down until everything is evenly mixed. Blend remaining 1/2 cup of olive oil in a steady stream, blend to a smooth consistency.

Pour sauce over 1 lb. linguine cooked al dente, toss until well coated. Sauce can be stored in a jar in refrigerator for several weeks by adding a layer of oil to cover top of pesto.

Origin: Sister-in-law, Patricia Miele

Lucy Yonnetti
Sgt. F. M. Bonanno Lodge #2549

Variation
2 1/2 cups fresh basil leaves, packed
omit parsley

Ellen Feigenbaum
Ft. Lauderdale Lodge #2263

Sauce Marino All' Ardea
(Cream Sauce with Bacon, Mushroom, Peas)

3 garlic cloves, sliced thin
1/2 lb. bacon, diced
1 cup heavy cream
1 lb. mushrooms, sliced thin
Parmesan cheese

1/2 medium onion, sliced
1 pkg. frozen peas
salt/pepper
1 lb. large pasta
(rigatoni, ziti, etc.)

Saute garlic, onion and bacon until bacon is cooked (do not crisp). Remove excess fat. Add mushrooms, salt and pepper, cook until mushrooms are limp. Add peas stir for 2-3 minutes, add heavy cream, bring to slow simmer, stir gently until thickened. Pour over cooked pasta.

Marie Lotito
Rev. Albert B. Palombo Lodge #2512

Eggplant Sauce

1 large eggplant	2 tbsp. capers
1/2 cup olive oil	1/2 cup black olives
1 large can plum tomatoes	(pitted/chopped)
(crushed)	2 garlic cloves, minced
salt/pepper	grated Parmesan cheese
8-10 fresh basil leaves, chopped	1 lb. Ziti or Spaghetti

Prepare eggplant
Wash eggplant; do not peel. Cut off stem; cut into lengthwise slices. Cut slices into 1" cubes. Heat 1/4 cup olive oil in a heavy skillet. When oil is quite hot, slip in as many eggplant cubes that will fit loosely in the pan. Let eggplant brown, then turn gently to brown on all sides. Do not salt.
Sauce
Heat 1 tbsp. olive oil in a heavy pan. Saute garlic lightly. Add tomatoes, salt and pepper and simmer for 20 minutes. Add fried eggplant, capers, olives and basil. Let simmer for 5 minutes. Pour sauce over cooked ziti.

Suzy Vargas
Sgt. F. M. Bonanno Lodge #2549

Variation
When you saute garlic, add 6 flat anchovies, 1 green pepper (chopped), and 1 medium onion (chopped). Add red pepper flakes and 1/4 cup fresh parsley (chopped) along with eggplant mixture to sauce.

Rose Abrams
Joseph A. Franzalia Lodge #2422
Dora Romero
Unita Lodge #2015

Besciamella
(White Sauce)

8 tbsp. unsalted butter	4 cups scalded milk
3/4 cup flour	1/2 tsp. grated nutmeg
1/2 tsp. salt	1/4 tsp. white pepper

Melt butter in a saucepan over low heat. With a wire whisk, blend in flour, salt and pepper, being careful not to scorch flour. Cook gently for a few minutes until blended, add milk all at once, stirring constantly. Continue to cook until sauce is thickened and smooth about 4 minutes. Add the nutmeg. Pour sauce into a bowl and whip it for a moment or two to cool and to give it more body. Cover with plastic wrap and let cool 10 minutes before serving.

Antoinette Zaffarano
Sgt. F. M. Bonanno Lodge #2549

PASTA

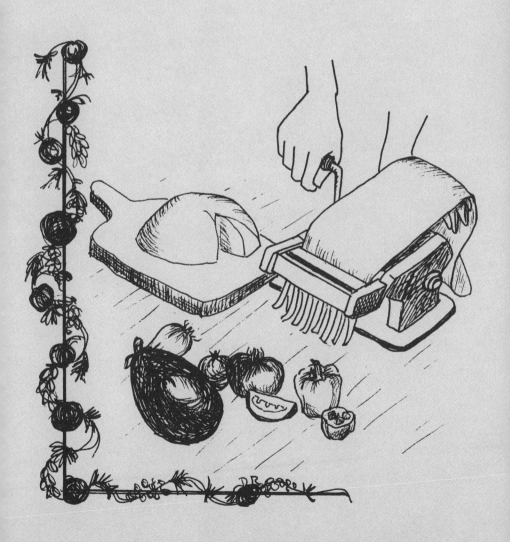

Pasta Fagioli I

1 (28 oz.) can crushed tomatoes	4 tbsp. olive oil
1 can cannellini beans, undrained	3 garlic cloves, minced
1 tsp. oregano	grated Parmesan cheese
1 lb. Ditalini, cooked firm	red pepper flakes
(drain, reserve 1 cup liquid)	salt/pepper

Saute garlic in olive oil, add tomatoes, salt and pepper; simmer 15 minutes. Add oregano and cannellini beans, simmer 10 minutes longer. Add cooked ditalini and some reserved water, if needed, stir around, let set 5 minutes. Serve with grated cheese and hot pepper.

Origin: Grandma Rosina Boniello

Rosalene Boniello Feller
Submitted by John Boniello
Sgt. F. M. Bonanno Lodge #2549

Pasta Fagioli II

1 medium onion, diced	1 can red Kidney beans
1/2 cup celery and leaves, diced	1 1/2 cups cooked Elbow macaroni
1 garlic clove, minced	2-4 tbsp. olive oil

Heat oil, saute onion, garlic and celery until transparent. Add red kidney beans, heat thoroughly. Add 1 1/2 cups of cooked elbow macaroni. Reheat and serve hot.

Origin: Anna Celiberti

Ann Tosti Goodman
Lake Worth/Boynton Beach Lodge #2304

Pasta and Ceci

2 small cans Garbanzo beans (ceci) 1 lb. Ditalini
2 large cans crushed tomatoes   1 cup water
3-4 garlic cloves, chopped   2 tbsp. oil
2 tbsp. basil or oregano

In a sauce pan, saute garlic in oil and add tomatoes, water, beans and basil, simmer 1 hour. Cook ditalini al dente and add to sauce.

Dianne Staffiero Barter
Key West Lodge #2436

Variation
1 garlic clove, minced   2 tbsp. parsley, chopped
1/4 cup olive oil   1 lb. Tubettini, cooked al dente
1 1/2 cups beef or chicken stock 4 tbsp. grated Parmesan cheese
2 small cans Ceci beans

Saute garlic in olive oil, add water or stock. Simmer 5-10 minutes, add tubettini and grated cheese, stir and let set for 5 minutes. Garnish with chopped parsley.

Renata Curcio Rathmann
La Nuova Sicilia Lodge #1251

Pasta and Peas

1 garlic clove   1/4 onion, diced
16 oz. can crushed tomatoes   1 tbsp. olive oil
2 (16 oz.) cans sweet peas   1 lb. Elbow pasta
1/2 tsp. oregano

Saute garlic and onion in oil. Add tomatoes and oregano, cook 15-20 minutes. Boil pasta al dente, drain; add peas. Pour sauce over pasta and let stand for 5 minutes.

The above recipe may be used with cannellini beans or lentils.

Raphaela Bruscino
Sunrise-Tamarac Lodge #2542

Spaghetti Aglio e Olio
(Spaghetti with Garlic and Oil)

1 lb. Spaghetti, cooked	1/4 cup fresh parsley, cut
1/2 cup olive oil	2 garlic cloves, minced
1/4 cup grated Parmesan cheese	salt/pepper

Keep 1 cup of spaghetti water.

Using small skillet or saucepan, put olive oil, garlic, parsley and pepper. Cook over low flame until garlic is slightly brown, do not overcook. Remove from heat and pour over cooked spaghetti. Sprinkle with grated cheese. Add some spaghetti water, if pasta is dry. Serves 4.

Palma Guarente
Coral Springs Lodge #2332

Variation

6 garlic cloves, chopped	1 lb. Linguine
10 cups of water	

In a pot big enough to cook pasta, add olive oil and garlic, simmer on low heat. Do not brown. Add water, salt, pepper and fresh parsley and continue to simmer for 10 minutes. Bring water to boil and add linguine, cook 12 minutes, remove from heat. Let rest in pot for 10-15 minutes. (Do not drain pasta.) Using a pasta serving spoon, remove pasta to soup dish and pour 1/4 cup of garlic water over pasta. Top with parmesan cheese. Serves 6 Non-Italians....3 Italians.

Origin: My own recipe.

Frank Terrana
Unita Lodge # 2015

Broccoli and Macaroni San Pierota

1 lb. Ziti	1 bunch broccoli
1 (28 oz.) can crushed tomatoes	hot pepper flakes
4 garlic cloves, sliced thin	3 oz. olive oil
salt/pepper	grated Parmesan cheese

Wash broccoli, cut into large flowerettes with stalks. Cook until crisp tender, drain. Reserve 2 cups of broccoli water. Use a large fry pan, saute garlic in olive oil until golden, pour over broccoli. Using same large fry pan, add tomatoes, salt and pepper and simmer slowly for 15 minutes.

Cook pasta al dente, drain and place in a deep dish. Toss pasta with tomato sauce, pour broccoli on top, add hot pepper flakes and grated Parmesan cheese.

Ann Borgia
Sgt. F. M. Bonanno Lodge #2549

Macaroni and Cauliflower

1 lb. Spaghetti
1 cup bread crumbs, seasoned
1/2 cup olive oil
1/4 tsp. hot pepper flakes, optional

1 head cauliflower
   (cut into floweretts)
1 large garlic clove, mashed

Steam cauliflower in a cup of water until tender, remove from heat, add seasoned bread crumbs, olive oil, garlic and hot pepper. Cover.

Boil spaghetti, drain all the water but 1 cup. Add water to cauliflower mixture. Pour over spaghetti and serve.

Origin: Sicily

Lucy Martino
John Paul I Lodge #2427

Spaghetti Pie

6 oz. Spaghetti
2 tbsp. butter/margarine
1/3 cup grated cheese
2 eggs, well-beaten
1 cup ricotta
1 lb. ground beef or sausage
1/2 cup onions, chopped

1/4 cup green peppers, chopped
1 (8 oz.) can tomatoes, chopped
1 (6 oz.) can tomato paste
1 tsp. sugar
1 tsp. oregano
1/2 tsp. garlic salt
1/2 cup mozzarella, shredded

Cook spaghetti according to package directions; drain. Stir butter or margarine into hot spaghetti. Stir in grated cheese and eggs. Form spaghetti mixture into a "crust" in a buttered 10" pie plate. Spread ricotta over bottom of spaghetti crust.

In skillet cook ground beef or sausage (remove casing), onion and green pepper until vegetables are tender and meat is browned. Drain off excess fat. Stir in undrained tomatoes, tomato paste, sugar, oregano, and garlic salt, heat through.

Turn meat mixture into spaghetti crust. Bake, uncovered, in 350 degree oven for 20 mintes. Sprinkle mozzarella cheese on top. Bake 5 minutes longer or until cheese melts. Serves 6.

Laura Spoto
La Nuova Sicilia Lodge #1251

Vermicelli with Zucchini

1 1/2 lbs. zucchini
   (sliced in 1/2" pieces)
1 garlic clove, minced
2 tbsp. fresh basil or
   (1/2 tsp. dry basil)
1 large can crushed tomatoes

1/4 cup olive oil
1 medium onion, chopped
2 cups water
1/2 lb. Vermicelli, broken in pieces
salt/pepper

Saute onion and garlic in oil until lightly brown, add tomatoes and simmer 10 minutes, add water and bring to boil. Add zucchini and basil and cook 10 minutes. Add Vermicelli and cook on low heat until tender, stirring occasionally. Serves 4.

Mary Scarfia
John Paul I Lodge #2427

Macaroni alla Michele

1 lb. ziti or penne
fresh grated horseradish

Marinara Sauce
grated Romano cheese

Boil macaroni according to directions with salt. Drain. Place in open casserole, add only enough sauce so that macaroni won't stick together. Add horseradish and cheese, cover with more sauce. Top with seasoned bread crumbs. Bake in 350 degree oven for 5-10 minutes.

Origin: Potenza, Italy - My father Michele Iannibelli always made this dish.

Edith Cuccinelli
Sgt. F. M. Bonanno Lodge #2549

Spaghetti con Le Sarde e Finocchio
(Spaghetti with Fennel and Sardines)

2 heads fresh fennel (anise)
  (about 1 cup leaves)
1/2 cup olive oil
1 large onion, chopped
3 garlic cloves, chopped
2 cans (6 oz.) tomato paste

4 cups water
2 cans (7 1/2 oz) sardines
  boneless/drained/halved
1 cup bread crumbs
1 lb. Spaghetti
salt/pepper

Cut leaves and top stems from fennel. (Reserve bulbs to be sliced and served at the end of the meal.) Wash and cook in 7 qts. of water for 5-6 minutes. Drain, reserving water to cook the pasta, then finely chop leaves and stems.

In a skillet heat 5 tbsp. olive oil and saute onion and garlic until golden, add paste, salt and pepper. Mix well saute a couple of minutes more. Add chopped fennel and 4 cups water. Bring to boil and let simmer for 30 minutes. Add sardines and cook 2-3 minutes.

Heat remaining oil in a skillet, add bread crumbs and slowly brown. (Reserve)

Cook pasta in fennel water until al dente. Drain. Place pasta in a large skillet with sauce over low heat, toss pasta and sauce adding browned bread crumbs. Let stand a few minutes before serving.

Philip Borgia
Sgt. F. M. Bonanno Lodge #2549

Variation

2 tbsp. olive oil
1 medium onion, chopped
1 cup water
1 cup toasted bread crumbs

1 can (2 oz.) flat anchovies
1 large can Condiments Completo
  (per pasta con sarde and
  finocchio, can be purchased
  in an Italian Specialty store)

Brown onion in olive oil, add anchovies, tomato paste and water, cook for 30 minutes. Add can of condiments and cook 30 minutes longer. Pour sauce over cooked spaghetti, sprinkle toasted bread crumbs on top.

Zina Guecia
John Paul I Lodge #2427

Seafood Pasta

1/2 cup olive oil
3 garlic cloves, minced
1/2 cup dry white wine
2 cups heavy cream
salt/pepper
2 tbsp. fresh parsley, chopped

3/4 lb. sea scallops
3/4 lb. shrimp, peeled/deveined
2 cans (6 1/2 oz.) chopped clams
cayenne pepper (optional)
mussels, chopped (optional)
1 lb. linguine, cooked al dente

In 5 qt. saucepan, heat oil, saute garlic, add wine, cream, cayenne pepper, salt and pepper. Bring to a slow boil. Add seafood, stir lower heat, cook until seafood is opaque. Add cooked drained linguine, toss to coat linguine for 2 minutes. Place on serving platter, garnish with parsley. Serve immediately.

Mary Dalfonzo
Sgt. F. M. Bonanno Lodge #2549

Filet of Fish with Linguine

1 large can plum tomatoes
  (cut in pieces)
1/3 cup fresh parsley, snipped
2 tbsp. capers
1 lb. Filet of Flounder
  (or fish of choice)
black pepper

1/4 cup olive oil
3 stalks celery, diced
1 large onion, sliced
1/3 cup green olives, sliced
1 lb. Linguine
grated cheese
dash of hot pepper, optional

In a sauce pan, simmer tomatoes and olive oil 20 minutes. Add celery, parsley, onions, capers, black pepper and olives, cook another 10 minutes. Lay fish on top of sauce simmer 10 minutes more. Turn off heat. Cook linguine, drain. While linguine is cooking put fish on plate, set aside. Mix pasta with sauce, place on platter. Put fish on top of pasta, add sauce, cheese and dash of hot pepper.

Origin: My mother's recipe

Jean D'Antonio
John Paul I Lodge #2427

Risotto with Shrimp and Capers

1/2 lb. fresh shrimp, devein/shell	1//2 cup butter
1 onion, chopped fine	2 garlic cloves, chopped fine
2 stalks celery, chopped fine	1 tbsp parsley, chopped
1 cup rice	salt/pepper
1 can (8 oz.) tomato sauce	chicken broth or water
2 tbsp. capers, drained	4 tbsp. grated Parmesan cheese

Slightly saute onion, celery and garlic in butter; add shrimp, parsley, salt and pepper, saute 5 minutes more. Add rice, salt and pepper, continue stirring until liquid is absorbed.

Blend tomato sauce with shrimp and enough hot broth or water to make 3 cups of liquid. Add rice with capers, stir until it comes to a boil. Pour into a casserole, bake uncovered in 350 degree oven for 30-40 minutes until liquid is absorbed and rice is tender. Sprinkle with cheese before serving.

Origin: Dominic "Papa" Rossi now deceased had his own Italian restaurant in San Francisco for over 50 years. He was widely known on the West Coast as one of the patriachs of fine Italian cuisine in this country. His daughter Antonia Rossi and foster son published a cookbook in his memory.

Jennie Caruso
John Paul I Lodge #2427

Shrimp and Rice

1 lb. med. size shrimp	2 cups rice
(clean and devein)	8 oz. crushed tomatoes
1 med. onion, chopped	1 garlic clove, minced
3 sprigs broad leaf parsley	2 oz. olive oil
(minced)	1/2 green pepper, chopped
salt/pepper	grated Parmesan cheese
6 cups water	

Heat oil in 8 qt. casserole with cover. Saute onion, green pepper and garlic on medium heat for 3 minutes then add crushed tomatoes. Cook for 5 minutes and add water. Bring to boil, stir in rice, salt, pepper and parsley. Return to boil then reduce heat to low, cook rice 20-25 minutes, stirring often. Add water if needed. When rice is cooked, add shrimp cook 3 minutes. Serve with grated cheese.

Philip Borgia
Sgt. F. M. Bonanno Lodge #2549

Risotto con Salsicce e Funghi
(Rice with Sausage and Mushrooms)

4 qts. chicken soup
3/4 lb. sweet sausage
1/2 lb. mushrooms, sliced
2 tbsp. olive oil
8 oz. dry wine
salt/pepper

1/2 cup butter
1 large onion, sliced
2 cups long grain rice
2-3 pinches of saffron
3/4 cup grated Parmesan cheese

Keep chicken soup on back burner on a low boil. Saute sausage in a little water on medium heat. Cook about 5 minutes. Remove, cut into 3/4" slices and set aside. Saute mushrooms in olive oil until brown, set aside.

In a 6 qt. pot, saute butter and onions until golden brown. Add sausage, mushrooms and wine, saute 2-3 minutes; add rice and saffron. Stir to mix, adding 1 cup of chicken soup. Stir and keep adding hot soup as needed while rice cooks. Stirring well so rice does not stick. Cook for 20-25 minutes. When rice is tender remove from heat, add grated cheese and serve. Serves 4-6. *"Better Next Day"*

Angelo Tacchi
Port St. Lucie Lodge #2594

Risotto Milanese
(Rice Milan Style)

6-8 cups Chicken broth
1 med. onion, chopped fine
3/4 cup white wine
1/2 cup Parmesan cheese

5 tbsp. butter
2 1/2 cups rice
1/2 tsp. saffron (optional)
salt/pepper

Heat broth in a sauce pan, set aside and keep hot. In a large sauce pan, saute onions with 4 tbsp. butter over medium heat. Add rice and mix well to coat rice with butter. Add wine, cook, stirring until wine has evaporated. Stir in enough broth to cover rice. Continue cooking and stirring rice and adding broth until rice is cooked, 15-20 minutes. Dissolve saffron with hot broth and add to rice mixture, stir in cheese and 1 tbsp. of butter. Serve hot.

Mary Dalfonzo
Sgt. F. M. Bonanno Lodge #2549
Lillian Ferrari Menza
Joseph A. Franzalia Lodge #2422

Arancini
(Rice Balls)

4 cups cooked rice
1 cup grated Parmesan cheese
1/2 cup tomato sauce
oil for frying

4 eggs, separated
(whites unbeaten for binding)
2 cups flavored bread crumbs

Filling
1/2 lb. ground chuck
garlic (fresh or powder)

1 cup peas
salt/pepper

Saute chop meat, break up well. Add garlic, salt, pepper, 1/4 cup sauce and peas. Simmer gently about 10 minutes. While mixture is cooling; add cheese and egg yolks to rice. Add remaining sauce a little at a time and just enough to add a little color to rice. Mix well. Shape into balls about the size of a small orange. Poke a hole in center and insert about 1 tsp. of filling. Pat ball with unbeaten egg white then roll in bread crumbs. Heat oil in deep frying pan and gently fry balls to a golden color. Drain on paper towel. Enjoy while nice and hot.

A family favorite for special occasions or holidays. My daughter made sure she followed Grandpa's recipe to carry on his traditional cooking. She sat with him before he died and recorded all his favorite recipes.

Origin: My Dad, Michael Leto brought this recipe from Messina, Sicily.

Sally Nelson
Federico Tesio Lodge #2619

Rice - Sausage Casserole

1 med. onion, chopped
1 lb. Italian sausage, remove casing
2/3 cup mozzarella, diced
1 tbsp. parsley, chopped

1 tbsp. olive oil
3 cups cooked rice
2 eggs, beaten

Saute onion in oil until tender. Add sausage, cook until browned. Pour off fat. Add rice and cheese, mix carefully. Transfer mixture to 2 qt. baking dish. Combine eggs and parsley and pour over rice-meat mixture. Bake 300 degrees for 30 minutes. Cut into squares to serve. Serves 6-8.

Origin: "A Family Favorite" from Northern Italy.

Lina Cassartelli Pellegatta
Jerry Barletta Lodge #2502

Arancini
(Sicilian Rice Balls)

2 cups rice, unwashed (use long
　grain enriched "sticky" rice)
3 eggs beaten
3/4 cup grated Parmesan cheese

1/4 lb. butter
salt/white pepper
oil for deep frying

Filling
2 garlic cloves, chopped
1 onion, chopped
2 tbsp. olive oil
1/2 lb. lean ground beef
salt/pepper
1 lb. mushrooms, sliced
　(optional)

1 cup crushed tomatoes
1 tsp. allspice, optional
1/4 cup white wine, optional
1 cup frozen peas
1/2 grated Parmesan cheese

To bind "Arancini", set aside 1 cup of flour, 2 eggs, 2 cups of fine bread crumbs.

Bring 5 cups of water and 1 tsp. salt to boil. Add rice, stirring well, cook about 15 minutes to al dente. Must not be cooked soft. Drain well. Add 3 eggs, grated cheese, butter, salt and white pepper; set aside to cool. (May be refrigerated overnight.)

Saute garlic and onion in olive oil, add meat, salt and pepper to brown slightly, add mushrooms, saute a few minutes more. Add tomatoes, allspice and wine, let simmer 15-20 minutes, add frozen peas. Turn up heat and stir well to thicken and dry for 5 minutes. Add grated cheese.

Form "Arancini" by placing 2-3 tablespoons of rice in the palm of your hand, make a dent in the middle, fill with a generous teaspoon of the meat filling. Cover the filling with more rice, sealing the edges and forming into a ball. Should be between 2 1/2" to 4" in diameter. No filling should show. Bind "Arancini" by rolling in flour, then in 2 beaten eggs, then in bread crumbs, set aside on a rack to dry as you make others.

Deep fry a few at a time in hot oil 375 degrees. Must be enough oil to cover them completely. Fry to a golden brown. Lift out with a slotted spoon and drain on paper towel. Set in a warm oven for 10 minutes to dry before serving.

Rose Van Saake
Sgt. F. M. Bonanno Lodge #2549
Dora Battaglia
Lake Worth/Bonton Beach Lodge #2304
Esther Messina
John Paul I Lodge #2427

Gnocchi with Potatoes

3 medium potatoes
2 egg yolks
1/2 tsp. salt

1 1/2 cups tomato sauce
1 cup grated Romano cheese
1 cup flour, approximately

For gnocchi, use a dry mealy type of potato. Boil potatoes in their jackets, peel and mash. (Do not pierce skin of potatoes while cooking.) Add egg yolks and salt; whip until fluffy. Add the flour and mix, then knead until smooth, adding more flour as necessary, to prevent sticking.

Divide the dough into six parts and shape each into a long roll about 1/2" in diameter. Flour hands and working board. Cut into 1" long pieces and press with thumb or fork. Sprinkle lightly with flour.

Add about a third of the gnocchi at a time to 6 qts. of boiling salted water, when gnocchi rise to top, cook about 5 minutes, remove with slotted spoon and place in heated bowl, keep warm. Repeat until all gnocchi have been cooked. Add one cup of tomato sauce and 1/2 cup of cheese and toss lightly. Turn onto a serving platter and pour the remaining sauce on top. Sprinkle with remaining cheese.

Coco Grosso
Sgt. F. M. Bonanno Lodge #2549

Gnocchi alla Romana

3 cups milk
1 cup Farina
4 tbsp. butter or margarine
dash nutmeg

2 eggs, beaten
1/2 cup grated Parmesan cheese
1/2 tsp. salt

Lightly butter a 13" x 9" x 2" baking pan. Heat the milk slightly in a 3 1/2 qt. heave saucepan. DO NOT BOIL. Sprinkle in Farina, cook over medium heat and stirring, until mixture is thick about 5 minutes. Remove from heat.

Stir in 2 tbsp. of butter, eggs, 1/4 cup Parmesan cheese, salt, and nutmeg; beat until smooth. Spread evenly in prepared baking dish or pan. Refrigerate until firm, about 3 hours.

To serve; cut the chilled mixture into 24 pieces, arrange pieces, overlapping, in shallow baking pan. Melt 2 tbsp. butter; and sprinkle over top with 1/4 cup Parmesan. Broil 4" from heat until hot and golden, about 5 minutes. Serves 8. **Buon Appetito!!**

Laura Spoto
La Nuova Sicilia Lodge #1251

Gnocchi di Ricotta
(Ricotta Dumplings)

1 lb. Ricotta	2 cups sifted flour
3 eggs	1 tbsp. melted butter
1/2 cup grated Parmesan cheese	

Mix all ingredients, knead until dough is formed. (If too soft add a little more flour.) Cover with a bowl and let stand one hour.

Sprinkle flour on your workboard and hands, take a tennis ball size of dough and roll gently with both hands and form a long rope of dough about 1" thick. Repeat this until you have used up dough. Cut the rolls into 1" long pieces and set aside to dry on a cloth covered surface. Do not place on formica. Cook gnocchi in a large pot of boiling salted water, water should not stop boiling. After they rise to top, gently boil 2-3 minutes more. Remove with slotted spoon and place in a large bowl, spooning meat sauce or your favorite sauce over each layer. Repeat until all gnocchi are cooked. Serves 4-6.

Anthony Simeone
John Paul I Lodge #2427
Virginia Minghella
Mike Accardi Lodge #2441

Gnocchi di Parmigiano
(Parmesan Dumplings)

1 1/2 cups milk	4 tbsp. butter or margarine
1 1/2 cups water	1/3 tsp. salt
1/2 cup Semolina flour	2 cups grated Parmesan cheese
1/2 cup melted butter	2 eggs
or margarine	

Mix together milk and water, butter or margarine and salt in a saucepan, bring to boil. Slowly add semolina, cook over medium heat until thick. Remove from heat, add 1 cup cheese and eggs, mixing well. Pour in a large platter, let cool. Mixture will harden. Cut into small squares.

Grease bottom of baking dish with melted butter or margarine. Put layer of squares on baking dish and sprinkle Parmesan cheese and melted butter, continue to make layers until all squares are used up. Season with salt and pepper. Bake in 375 degree oven about 1/2 hour.

Origin: My Mom's recipe

Margaret Scarfia
John Paul I Lodge #2427

Connie's Fried Ziti

12 oz. uncooked ziti or ditali	1 tbsp. butter
2 tbsp. olive oil	3 whole scallions, chopped
1 large garlic clove, minced	1 tsp. salt
1/4 tsp. coarse pepper	1 tsp. oregano
1/2 cup Marinara sauce	3/4 cup mozzarella, grated

Cook ziti or ditali, drain and refrigerate to chill. Transfer ziti, if used, to a board and chop coarsely.

In a large skillet, heat butter and olive oil, add scallions and garlic, saute briefly. Add chopped ziti or ditali and cook, stirring and shaking the pan back and forth, until pasta is golden brown. Stir in salt, pepper, oregano and sauce mixing well. Transfer to shallow baking pan and scatter grated mozzarella evenly over the top.

Bake in a preheated oven 400 degrees for 10-15 minutes to melt cheese and brown, or run under broiler (watching carefully) for about 5 minutes. Serve at once.

Connie Agliardi
Jerry Barletta Lodge #2502

Rigatoni Vodka

4 cups Marinara sauce	1 lb. Rigatoni, cooked
4 1/2 oz. Vodka	3 oz. butter
2/3 cup grated cheese	9 slices mozzarella
6 oz. proscuitto, chopped	3 egg yolks
pepper	1 pt. heavy cream

Place butter and proscuitto in pan allow to simmer, add vodka.
NOTE: When adding vodka be extremely careful, remove pan from stove, "this could flame." Allow to simmer. Add heavy cream, marinara sauce, pepper, grated cheese, mozzarella and mix together with Rigatoni. When serving add extra sauce on plate and garnish with parsley.

Margy Marrapodi
Port Charlotte Lodge #2507

Orzo Primavera

2 cups Orzo pasta
1/2 cup red peppers, diced
1 cup frozen peas
1 tsp. butter or margarine
1/2 cup chicken broth
1/4 tsp. white pepper

1 lb. thin spear asparagus
(cut 1" pieces)
1 tbsp. olive oil
3 garlic cloves
1 tsp. lemon peel, grated
1/2 cup Parmesan cheese

Bring 3 qts. of salted water to a rapid boil. Add pasta and boil for 5 minutes. Add asparagus and boil an additional 4 minutes. Drain. Place in serving bowl. Melt butter and oil together in medium skillet over moderate heat. Add garlic and saute until golden brown. Be careful not to burn. Add diced peppers, stir. Add peas and saute for 1 minute, add chicken broth, lemon peel and white pepper. Boil for 1 minute. Pour over pasta, toss quickly. Sprinkle with Parmesan cheese. Serves 4-6.

Rosalene Boniello Feller
Submitted by John Boniello
Sgt. F. M. Bonanno Lodge #2549

Baked Mostaccioli with Sausage and Peppers

1 lb. sweet or hot sausage
(casings removed)
1 green pepper, thinly sliced
1 med. onion, sliced
(separate into rings)
4 cups Marinara sauce

1 cup water
1 lb. Mostaccioli
(cook 8 minutes, drain)
1 lb. mozzarella, shredded
1/2 cup Parmesan cheese

In large skillet, brown sausage, pepper and onion over medium-high heat 6 to 8 minutes, stirring frequently. Add Marinara sauce and water. Bring to boil. Reduce heat and simmer 10 minutes. Spread 1 cup sauce in bottom of 13" x 9" x 2" baking dish. Top with half the Mostaccioli, half of the mozzarella and Parmesan cheese. Spread 2 cups of sauce then layer remaining, pasta, sauce and mozzarella. Bake in 350 degree oven for 30 minutes or until heated. Serves 6-8.

Teresa Mirabella
Unita Lodge # 2015

Manicotti

Crepes
4 eggs	2 cups water
2 tbsp. oil	dash of salt
2 cups flour	

Filling
3 lb. can ricotta	2 eggs
2 tbsp. parsley, chopped	1/2 cup Romano cheese
1/2 lb. mozzarella, shredded	Marinara Sauce

Make crepes like pancake batter, beat until smooth. Use 6" skillet with a few drops of oil. Pour a large tablespoon of batter in pan, just to cover bottom of pan turn quickly for about half a minute and remove. Trick is to keep pan hot and do not brown, they look raw when they are done. Pile one on top of each other until ready to stuff.

Combine all filling ingredients, set aside. Cover bottom of baking pans with Marinara sauce, set aside.

Manicotti: Spread out crepes, place 1 tablespoon of ricotta filling on the center of each, gently roll leaving ends open. Repeat process until all ingredients are used. Place manicotti side by side in baking pan. Spread more sauce on top, sprinkle with grated cheese. Bake 20-25 minutes.

Mary Baldassare
John Paul I Lodge #2427
Virginia Papale
Sunrise-Tamarac Lodge #2542

Fettuccini Fantastic

1 pkg. extra long Fettuccini	1 lb. fresh spinach leaves
(cooked al dente)	(washed and drained)
4 chicken breasts, boned	2 tbsp. olive oil
2 1/2 cups Marinara sauce	salt/pepper
2 cups Ricotta cheese	grated Italian cheese

Heat olive oil, saute chicken breasts, set aside. Roll up cooked Fettucini (nests) arrange in a casserole. Lay spinach leaves on top, then place chicken breasts over spinach leaves. Pour 2 cups tomato sauce over all. Sprinkle ricotta cheese on top. Bake in a moderate oven, covered, for 15-20 minutes. Uncover and bake an additional 10-15 minutes until chicken is tender. Serve with grated cheese and sauce. Serves 4.

Origin: Friends in Connecticut

Rita J. Ricci
John Paul I Lodge #2427

Polenta

Sauce

1 lb. Italian sausage
  (remove casing)
1/2 lb. mushrooms, sliced
2 tbsp. olive oil
1 (28 oz.) can crushed tomatoes
salt/pepper

Polenta

1 cup corn meal
1 cup water, cold
grated Parmesan cheese

Heat oil in skillet, add mushrooms and sausage stirring until lightly browned. Stir in tomatoes, salt and pepper. Simmer for 30 minutes.

Bring 3 cups of water and 1 1/2 tsp. of salt to boil. Combine and blend corn meal and 1 cup of water. Gradually add blended corn meal to boiling water, stirring at all times. Cook until thick. Reduce heat, cover pan and cook 5 more minutes. Transfer cooked corn meal to platter and top with sauce. Sprinkle with cheese.

Margaret Scarfia
John Paul I Lodge #2427

Variation:

Use meatballs in the sauce or ground beef in place of sausage.

Pauline Salciccioli
Unita Lodge #2015

Lasagne Rollatine
(Spinach Filling)

1 lb. Lasagne noodles
1 lb. ricotta
1 1/2 cup grated Parmesan cheese
salt/pepper

3 pkg. frozen chopped spinach
  (cook and drain well)
1/4 lb. butter, melted
Marinara sauce

Preheat oven to 350 degrees.

Prepare lasagne according to package directions. Mix spinach, cheeses, butter, salt and pepper. Place a few tablespoons of Marinara sauce on bottom of 9" X 12" baking dish. Spread each noodle thinly with spinach filling, roll noodles and place seam edge down in pan. Top with Marinara sauce and repeat with another layer. Bake in oven for 40 minutes or until hot.

Laura Spoto
La Nuova Sicilia Lodge #1251

Cheese Stuffed Shells Florentine

3-4 cups Marinara sauce	1 pkg. frozen spinach, chopped
2 lbs. Ricotta	1 egg
2 tbsp. grated cheese	1 pkg. (12 oz.) jumbo shells

Pour Marinara sauce into sauce pan, heat. Spoon one cup sauce into bottom of a large roasting pan or 1/2 cup into each of two 2 qt. baking dishes. Cook spinach as directed, drain and mix with ricotta cheese, egg and grated cheese. Cook shells according to package directions, drain. Using a teaspoon, fill each shell with cheese mixture. Arrange shells in single layers on sauce in roasting pan. Bake at 350 degrees for 15-20 minutes. Serve with reserved hot Marinara sauce. Serves 6.

Laura Spoto
La Nuova Sicilia Lodge #1251

Meat and Spinach Filling for Shells

2 lbs. ground chuck	2 stalks celery, chopped fine
1/2 medium onion, chopped fine	2 tbsp. parsley, chopped
1 pkg. frozen chopped spinach	1 garlic clove, crushed
(cooked/drained)	3/4 cup Romano cheese
1 cup bread crumbs	4 eggs, well-beaten
1/2 tsp. sage	1/2 tsp. basil
2 tsp. salt	3/4 tsp. pepper
1 lb. large shells	oil for frying

Your favorite tomato sauce -

Put a little oil in frying pan and saute celery, onion and garlic. Add meat, cook until meat is brown, add spinach; stir for several minutes, turn off heat, add remaining ingredients and mix well. Cook shells al dente drain and fill. Arrange filled shells in a layer of sauce in a baking dish. Bake 350 degrees 15 minutes.

Millie Pietrini
Young Italians Lodge #2256

Lasagne

2-4 tbsp. Olive oil	1 large can tomato puree
1 medium onion, sliced	1 (6 oz.) can tomato paste
3 garlic cloves, sliced	1/2 cup water
1 1/2 lbs. ground beef	salt/pepper
1/2 lb. mozzarella, sliced	3 tsp. sugar, optional
1 lb. pork shoulder	1 tsp. baking soda, optional
1 lb. Lasagne noodles	

Heat oil, add pork, salt and pepper, brown thoroughly on all sides. Remove and set aside. Add onion, garlic, ground beef, salt and pepper, stir and cook until beef is well browned. Add puree, paste, water, sugar and baking soda. Stir, let simmer for 5 minutes. Add pork and continue to cook about 1 hour until pork is fork tender.

Ricotta Filling

2 lbs. ricotta	1 cup Parmesan cheese
1 tbsp. parsley, chopped	salt/pepper

Mix ricotta filling ingredients and set aside.

Boil lasagne al dente, drain. Coat bottom of a baking dish with 1/2 cup of sauce, arrange lasagne layers, alternating with sauce and ricotta. Over last layer of lasagne add sauce then layer with mozzarella slices. Bake in preheated oven 375 degrees for 20 minutes. Serve Pork as a second course.

Comments: I often make tiny meat balls, drop them in the sauce and layer them in the lasagne. Enjoy.

Katie Copuzelo
Sunrise-Tamarac Lodge #2542

Palm Sunday Macaroni

1 lb. ziti	2 cups tomato sauce
2/3 cups seasoned bread crumbs	1/2 cup Romano cheese
1/2 cup walnuts, chopped	salt/pepper

All ingredients are to individual taste. Cook ziti al dente. Stir in 1 cup sauce. Add mixture of seasoned bread crumbs, cheese and chopped walnuts. Cover with sauce and serve.

Traditional to my family. Served on Palm Sunday.

Origin: Potenza, Italy

Cookey Colonna
Submitted by Edith Cuccinelli
Sgt. F. M. Bonanno Lodge #2549

Pastiera Dolce
(Sweet Pasta)

1/2 lb. ziti	3 eggs
1 lb. ricotta	1 tsp. cinnamon
3 tbsp. sugar	1/2 tsp. salt
nutmeg to taste	

Cook pasta al dente and then blend all ingredients together. Place in a 2 quart greased casserole. Bake 40 minutes in 375 degree oven until center is dry.

Traditional Ash Wednesday and Good Friday dish.

Origin: Abruzzi, Italy

M. Palma Guarente
Coral Springs Lodge #2332

Pastiera di Carnivale
(Shrove Tuesday Baked Fettuccine and Sausage)

1 lb. fettuccine	10 eggs
1 lb. sweet sausage	1 cup Parmesan cheese
1 lb. ricotta	1 tsp. coarse ground pepper
	1 tbsp. butter, melted

Cook fettuccine al dente, rinse in cool water, drain and set aside. Broil sausage until cooked, then slice in 1" pieces.

In a bowl, mix ricotta, eggs, parmesan cheese and black pepper. Add sausage and cooked pasta, blending well. Preheat an oblong glass pyrex dish with melted butter. Pour Pastiera into the hot dish and bake at 350 degrees, 25-30 minutes until golden brown and eggs are set.

A tradition in our family to serve this dish on Shrove Tuesday.

Origin: Grandma, Rosina Boniello, San Nazzaro, Italy

Rose Marie Boniello
Sgt. F. M. Bonanno Lodge #2549

Secondi Piatti/
Second Courses

Beef Heart alla Soffritto

1 Beef heart
1/4 tsp. oregano
salt/pepper
1 medium onion, chopped
2 tbsp. olive oil

1 can tomato paste
1/2 tsp. basil
1 garlic clove, chopped
1 1/2 cups water for sauce

Wash heart in salted water, cover with water and simmer until fork tender. Drain and let cool. Cut and remove any membranes and fat. Cut heart into small cubes.

In a sauce pan, heat oil, saute onion and garlic until soft. Add heart, tomato paste, 1 1/2 cups of water and spices. Stir to blend, simmer covered for 1/2 hour, adding water as needed. Serve with crunchy bread and salad.

Old time favorite.

Mary Sorci
John Paul I Lodge #2427

Tripe

1 bunch of parsley, chopped
4 garlic cloves, chopped
1 tsp. nutmeg
1 small can tomato sauce
6 lemons, squeezed

4 large onions, sliced
salt/pepper
1 lb. margarine
4 lbs. Tripe
1/2 lb. grated Parmesan cheese

Saute parsley, onions, garlic, salt and pepper with margarine. When onions are soft, add tomato sauce, let simmer for 10 minutes.

Cover tripe in plenty of water and cook about 2 hours, until tender. Drain the tripe and cut in 1" strips then pour lemon juice over top and let stand for 10 minutes. Combine sauce and tripe, pour into a large baking pan and sprinkle 1/2 of the cheese over all. Mix well, then sprinkle remaining cheese on top, cover with aluminum foil and bake 350 degrees for 1 hour.

A rich delicious recipe - Buon Appetito.

Origin: My mother Alberta Di Corte, Burgio, Sicily

Laura D. Spoto
La Nuova Sicilia Lodge #1251

Trippa

2 lbs. honeycomb tripe
2 cups onion, chopped
1/4 cup white wine

2 cups celery, chopped
1 tsp. salt
4 tbsp. olive oil

Sauce
2 cups chicken broth
3 garlic cloves, chopped
2 tbsp. parsley, chopped
1/2 tsp. cinnamon
black pepper to taste

3 tbsp. tomato paste
1 tsp. basil
1 tsp. salt
1/2 tsp. nutmeg
4 tbsp. Parmesan cheese

Wash tripe amd simmer in 4 qts. of water with 1/4 tsp. salt, 1 cup celery and 1 cup onions for 2 hours. Drain and cool, then cut into 1/2" strips.

In large fry pan with cover, pour in oil, add remaining celery and onions, saute 5 minutes. Add tripe to celery and onions. Stir fry, 5 minutes. Add wine and cook an additional 5 minutes. Add sauce ingredients and simmer until tender for 1 1/2-2 hours. Serve over frisella or rice. Before serving sprinkle mixture with Parmesan cheese.

Origin: Sicily

Rose Van Saake
Sgt. F. M. Bonanno Lodge #2549

Tripe Florentine

2 lbs. tripe
2 carrots, grated
1 onion, chopped
3 garlic cloves, crushed
1/2 cup beef broth
1 tsp. oregano
1/2 tsp. basil
2 pieces lemon peel, 1" long

4 tbsp. olive oil
1/2 cup celery, chopped
1/2 cup parsley, chopped
1 8-oz. can tomato sauce
1/2 cup dry red wine
1 bay leaf, crushed
salt/pepper
1/2 cup Parmesan cheese

Parboil tripe for about 30 minutes. Drain and cool, then slice into 1/2" wide pieces.

In a 6 qt. pot, heat 2 tablespoons of oil, saute tripe very quickly then remove. Add remaining oil, carrots, celery, onion, parsley and garlic, stir and saute 2-3 minutes. Add tomato sauce, soup broth, wine, oregano, bay leaf, basil, salt, pepper and lemon peel. Simmer for a few minutes then add tripe.

Cook on stove, covered for 1 1/2 hours, until tender. Or bake in a moderate oven. Serve with Parmesan cheese over pasta and pass lots of crunchy Italian bread.

Rose Malzone
Ft. Lauderdale Lodge #2263

Tripe with Potatoes and Mushrooms

3 lbs. tripe
2 garlic cloves, crushed
1 onion, chopped
4 tbsp. olive oil
salt/pepper
grated Parmesan cheese
1/2 tsp. oregano

1 large can crushed tomatoes
3-4 large potatoes,
  (cut into large cubes)
1 lb. mushrooms, sliced
water as needed
hot pepper flakes, optional

Wash tripe - remove all visible fat and cut into 1/2" strips. Saute tripe in olive oil over low heat, stir for 5 minutes. Add onions, salt and pepper and saute until onion is soft. Add tomatoes, oregano, water to cover tripe and let simmer, covered over low heat for 2 1/2 hours. Stir often, adding water as needed to cover 1" over tripe. After 2 1/2 hours add potatoes and mushrooms. Adjust seasonings, add water to cover vegetables, cook slowly 15-20 minutes until potatoes are fork tender.

Pour into soup bowls, sprinkle with hot pepper and grated Parmesan cheese. Serve with fresh baked bread and a salad.

Origin: My friend Sina Henry - Messina, Italy

Rose Marie Boniello
Sgt. F. M. Bonanno Lodge #2549

Veal Chops Pizzaiola

6 Loin or Rib Veal chops
  (1/2" thick)
1/4 cup olive oil
1 tsp. oregano
1/2 tsp. parsley, chopped

1 28-oz. can plum tomatoes
  (crushed)
2 garlic cloves, sliced
salt/pepper

In a large fry pan with a tight fitting lid, heat oil and brown veal chops on both sides with salt and pepper.

Combine all other ingredients and pour over browned chops, cover and cook over low heat for 45 minutes.

Mary Sorci
John Paul I Lodge #2427

Veal Scalloppine

1 lb. Veal cutlets, sliced thin (cut into 3" squares)	3 tbsp. butter
	2 garlic cloves, sliced
1 tbsp. flour	pinch of sage
1 small onion, sliced	pinch of nutmeg
1/2 cup dry white wine	1/2 cup tomato puree
1/4 lb. mushrooms, sliced	1 tbsp. stuffed green olives
salt/pepper	(sliced)

Saute mushrooms in 1 tbsp. of butter, set aside. In same pan, saute garlic in 2 tbsp. butter until light golden color then discard garlic, and add veal. Saute veal until brown, then sprinkle with flour, salt, pepper, sage and nutmeg. Add onions, wine and tomatoe puree. Cover and cook about 20 minutes or until tender. Stir several times while cooking. When veal is tender add mushrooms and olives, cook about 5-7 minutes. Add a little wine or water if veal sauce is too thick.

Serve over pasta or rice.

Millie Pietrini
Young Italians Lodge #2256

Ossobuco
(Veal Shanks)

8 Veal shanks	1/2 cup flour
3/4 cup butter or margarine	3/4 cup dry white wine
8 large tomatoes (peeled and chopped)	2 large garlic cloves, crushed
	1 1/2 tsp. grated lemon rind
3 tbsp. parsley, chopped	salt/pepper

Roll shanks in flour seasoned with salt and pepper. Melt butter in a large sauce pan, add veal and brown on all sides. Add wine and cook over low heat for 10 minutes. Add tomatoes and garlic. Cover and simmer about 1 1/2 hours. Before serving sprinkle with grated lemon rind and chopped parsley. Serves 4-8.

Anthony Simeone
John Paul I Lodge #2427

Ossobuco Milanese
(Veal Shanks Milan Style)

6 Veal shanks, (cut 2" thick)
1/3 cup olive oil
1 carrot, chopped
3/4 cup dry white wine
2 tbsp. parsley, chopped
salt/pepper

1/2 cup flour
1 medium onion, chopped fine
1 celery stalk, chopped
1 28-oz. can crushed tomatoes
2 garlic cloves, chopped

Sprinkle veal with flour. Heat oil in large pot, add veal and brown on all sides over medium heat then remove veal. Add onion, celery, carrot and saute until lightly brown. Return veal to pot, stir in wine and tomatoes. Cover pot and simmer 1 1/2 hours until meat falls from bone. Add parsley, garlic, salt and pepper. Arrange meat and sauce on warm platter, garnish with parsley. Makes 6 servings.

The perfect accompaniment for this dish is Risotto Milanese.

Cecilia K. Andrews
Joseph A. Franzalia Lodge #2422
Mary Dalfonzo
Sgt. F. M. Bonanno Lodge #2549

Ossobuco al Forno
(Baked Veal Shanks)

8 Veal shanks (cut 2" thick)
1/2 cup wine (White or Rose)
1/2 cup seasoned flour
 (1/2 cup flour, salt,
 pinch of rosemary, oregano,
 thyme, 1 tsp. of paprika,
 pepper)
2-4 fresh basil leaves, chopped

2 cups tomatoes, chopped
1 cup chicken broth
1/4 cup lemon juice
1/2 tsp. cinnamon
1/2 cup olive oil
1/2 tsp. garlic powder
2 tsp. margarine

Dust shanks in seasoned flour and brown in olive oil and margarine. Place in a baking dish and add tomatoes, wine, chicken broth, garlic powder, fresh basil, cinnamon and lemon juice.

Bake at 375 degrees for 1 hour or until tender and brown. Serve with rice and salad. Serves 8.

Marissa Trimarchi
Sgt. F. M. Bonanno Lodge #2549

Veal Spedini

1 lb. Veal cutlets, sliced thin (cut in 3" pieces)	2 cups plain bread crumbs (pan browned*)
3 garlic cloves, chopped	4 tbsp. butter
2 tbsp. tomato juice	salt/pepper
2 tbsp. fresh parsley, minced	1 small onion, minced
2 eggs, beaten	1/2 cup olive oil
1 1/2 cups plain bread crumbs	1 large onion, quartered

Pan brown bread crumbs - melt 4 tbsp. butter in a large skillet, add 2 cups of bread crumbs, stir over moderate heat until brown.

Stuffing
Mix 2 cups of pan browned bread crumbs with garlic, salt, pepper, parsley, minced onion and tomato juice.

Place veal pieces flat; put a tablespoon of bread stuffing on center and roll. Use skewers; alternating, veal and onion until filled. Then place skewer in beaten egg and roll in bread crumbs. Saute in oil until cooked on both sides.

Dora Battaglia
Lake Worth/Boynton Beach Lodge #2304

Scalloppine di Vitello alla Romana
(Roman Veal Scallopini)

1 1/2 lbs. veal, pounded thin (cut in 3" pieces)	8 tbsp. butter
3/4 lbs. mushrooms, sliced	2/3 cup dry white wine
1 small onion, finely chopped	salt/pepper
1 garlic clove	grated Parmesan cheese
	2 lbs. fresh tomatoes, chopped

Heat 5 tablespoons of butter in skillet, saute mushroom until golden brown, about 5 minutes. Add onions and garlic, cook until onion is golden. Add tomatoes, salt, simmer; cover, stirring occasionally for 30 minutes.

Wipe veal with damp paper towels sprinkle with salt and pepper. Heat 3 tbsp. butter in another skillet. Add veal, a few pieces at a time, cook until lightly browned on both sides, about 5 minutes. Remove garlic from sauce and pour over veal, simmer, covered for 5 minutes. Sprinkle with Parmesan cheese. Serves 6.

Buon Appetito!

Laura Spoto
La Nuova Sicilia Lodge #1251

Veal and Peppers

1 lb. Veal, cubed
1 green pepper, sliced
2 sprigs Italian parsley, minced
1 can tomatoes, crushed
Parmesan cheese

1 medium onion, sliced
1 garlic clove, minced
4 tbsp. Olive oil
salt/pepper

Saute veal in a 6 qt. casserole with oil until brown; add minced garlic, parsley, salt and pepper and stir for 3 minutes. Add crushed tomatoes and bring to a boil. Cover pot and simmer on low heat for 45 minutes. Add onions and peppers, stir and continue to cook for 15 minutes, add salt and pepper to taste.

I serve my family the veal and peppers over Fettuccine topped with Parmesan cheese.

Phil Borgia
Sgt. F. M. Bonanno Lodge #2549

Veal Marsala with Artichoke Hearts

4 Veal cutlets, sliced thin
2 tbsp. fresh parsley, chopped
salt/pepper
1/4-1/2 cup Marsala dry wine
4 tbsp. Olive oil
1 cup Beef broth

1/2 cup bread crumbs
1 small onion, sliced
1-(6 oz.) jar Artichoke Hearts
 (marinated)
1 egg, beaten
1/4 lb. mushrooms, sliced

Dip veal into egg then bread crumbs on both sides, saute until golden brown. Place breaded veal cutlet side by side in baking pan coated with oil.

On top of veal cutlets, place contents of artichoke jar, onions, mushrooms, salt, pepper, parsley. Pour beef broth and Marsala wine over cutlets. Cover with aluminum foil. Bake 450 degrees for 15 minutes, remove foil, lower heat to 350 degrees, bake additional 15-20 minutes.

Dia De Carolis
Submitted by Flo Lendino
Lake Worth/Boynton Beach Lodge #2304

Shucheda
(Ground Veal and Eggs)

Veal mixture
2 lbs. veal ground
2 eggs, beaten
1/2-2/3 cup bread crumbs
salt/pepper

Egg Mixture
20 eggs
3/4-1 cup Romano cheese
1/2 cup parsley, chopped
salt/pepper

4 cups chicken broth

Veal: Add bread crumbs, eggs, salt and pepper to ground veal. Mix to blend well. Shape into 3 large meat balls, set aside.

Egg: Slowly beat eggs in a mixer, adding cheese, parsley, salt and pepper, set aside. In an oblong baking pan (8"x 11" x 5") pour chicken broth to a depth of 1". Place meat balls in broth, evenly spaced. Then pour egg mixture into pan. Bake 325 degrees until eggs are firm, about 15-25 minutes. When cooked serve slices of veal and eggs, adding some chicken broth to moisten.

Traditional to my family. This dish is served on Easter Sunday as a soup course.

Origin: Sicily

Josephine Miracola
Ft. Lauderdale Lodge #2263

Veal Parmesan ☆

1 lb. Veal, sliced 1/4" thick
2 eggs, beaten
3/4 cups bread crumbs
4 tbsp. parsley, chopped
Olive oil

1/4 cup Parmesan cheese
2 1/2 cups tomato sauce
3/4 lb. mozzarella, sliced
salt/pepper

Cut veal into 4 serving pieces and pound slightly. Combine bread crumbs, parsley, Parmesan cheese, salt and pepper. Dip veal into eggs then bread crumbs coating both sides. Heat oil; saute veal until golden brown.

Spread 1/2 cup tomato sauce on the bottom of a baking pan. Arrange veal on sauce and pour additional sauce on top. Sprinkle with Parmesan cheese. Bake 350 degrees for 15-20 minutes. Remove from oven and top each piece of veal with slices of mozzarella. Bake 5 minutes until cheese melts.

Charles Fabozzi
La Famiglia Lodge #2508

Coniglio al Forno
(Baked Rabbit)

4 lb. rabbit, cut in pieces	3 garlic cloves, crushed
1/2 cup parsley, chopped	1/2 cup Parmesan cheese
1 medium onion, sliced	2 tbsp. bread crumbs
1/3 cup olive oil	2 lbs. potatoes, peeled
salt/pepper	(cut in quarters)
4 fresh plum tomatoes, crushed	

Combine onion, 2 tablespoons of olive oil, salt, pepper, 2 crushed tomatoes and 1/4 cup parsley. Spread evenly in a large baking pan.

Mix garlic, 1/4 cup cheese, remainder of parsley, salt, pepper, 3 tbsp. oil and bread crumbs to form a paste. Make a slit in each piece of rabbit and stuff the bread crumb mixture into the pockets. Arrange rabbit in the baking pan with potato quarters and remaining tomatoes. Sprinkle salt, pepper and cheese then drizzle olive oil over top.

Cover pan and bake 350 degrees for 1 hour and 15 minutes (basting every 1/2 hour). Remove cover and bake an additional 15 minutes.

Traditional to my family, this dish is served on "Pasquetta" the Monday after Easter. Years ago my family and friends would gather for a picnic in the country and bake the rabbit in a clay pot surrounded by hot coals.

Origin: *My mother, Lucrezia DeFilippis*
Triggiano, Bari

Antonette Zaffarano
Sgt. F. M. Bonanno Lodge #2549

Coniglio Imbottito con Prosciutto
(Rabbit Stuffed with Prosciutto)

5 lbs. rabbit, whole
3 stalks fresh dill
4 bacon slices or
  (pancetta)

3 garlic cloves, chopped
1 lb. piece of prosciutto
fresh ground pepper

Debone the rabbit leaving the outer skin intact. Lay flat, then layer dill, bacon and garlic. Place the prosciutto on top. Grind pepper over all. Roll the rabbit like a braciole and tie securely with kitchen string. Place in an oiled baking pan, roast 350 degrees for 1-1 1/2 hours. Serve sliced as a hot appetizer or second course with salad.

Origin: My cousin Mario Giuliani, Battipaglia, Italy

Rose Marie Boniello
Sgt. F. M. Bonanno Lodge #2549

Coniglio Potacchio
(Rabbit in Red Wine, Marchigiana Style)

1 large Rabbit, dressed
2-3 tbsp. Olive oil
salt/pepper
1/2 cup red wine vinegar

2 tbsp. rosemary leaves
16 garlic cloves,
  (peeled to the last skin)

Cut rabbit into small pieces. Use frypan with a tight cover that will take the whole rabbit. Heat olive oil, add rabbit, salt and pepper. On high heat, stir to brown rabbit on all sides quickly. Add rosemary leaves, garlic and vinegar. Lower heat to simmer gently, keep covered. When rabbit is fork tender (25-30 minutes), remove cover. Put on high heat to reduce liquid. Turn rabbit pieces to coat in the pan juices and glaze. Serve in a heated platter, pour remaining juices and garlic over top.

Pop the garlic cloves onto slices of crusty bread, spread like butter and enjoy.

Origin: My father, Raul Giuliani

Rose Marie Boniello
Sgt. F. M. Bonanno Lodge #2549

Rabbit alla Siciliana

4 lbs. rabbit
  (cut into serving pieces)
1 garlic clove, crushed
2 tbsp. fresh parsley, chopped
1/2 tsp. basil, crushed
1/2 cup red wine

3 tbsp. olive oil
2 tbsp. butter
1 medium onion, chopped
1 large can Italian tomatoes
  (crushed/undrained)
salt/pepper

Wash rabbit, pat dry with paper towels. Heat oil and butter in dutch oven, add rabbit a few pieces at a time and brown well on all sides. Remove, set aside. Add onions and garlic to dutch oven and saute until golden brown, about 5 minutes. Add parsley, tomatoes, salt, pepper and basil and bring to a boil, reduce heat and simmer, uncovered, 20 minutes. Add browned rabbit and wine; simmer, covered, 45-50 minutes or until rabbit is tender.

Serve rabbit with polenta or spaghetti. Garnish with chopped parsley. Serves 6-8.

Laura Spoto
La Nuova Sicilia Lodge #1251

Rabbit

1 small rabbit, cut into pieces
2 tbsp. olive oil
salt/pepper
1 garlic clove, chopped

2 slices prosciutto or bacon
1 tbsp. parsley, chopped
1 cup dry wine
5 fresh tomatoes, peeled
  (chopped)

Place rabbit in frying pan with oil. Add salt, pepper and garlic and brown slowly. When well browned, add prosciutto or bacon and parsley. Continue browning a few minutes. Add wine and cook until wine has evaporated. Add tomatoes and about 1/2 cup of water, lower heat and cook slowly until meat is tender (about 1 hour). Serves 4.

Rose Marie Tufarella
Sunrise-Tamarac Lodge #2542

Polpettine ⭐
(Meatballs)

1 1/2 lbs. ground beef	1 tbsp. parsley, chopped
1 egg	1 garlic clove, minced
1/4 cup Parmesan cheese	1 hard roll softened in milk
salt/pepper	

Mix all ingredients thoroughly. Shape into small balls about 2" in diameter and drop into simmering tomato sauce. Cook slowly 20-25 minutes, stir carefully.

Variation: Meatballs may be browned in hot olive oil, then dropped into simmering sauce.

Variation: Place meatballs on an oiled broiler pan, turn carefully as they brown.

Renata Curcio Rathmann
La Nuova Sicilia Lodge #1251

Meat and Potato Stew

2-3 lbs. round steak or top round	1/4 cup olive oil
(cut into 1" cubes)	1/2 tsp. oregano
6 oz. can tomato paste	1/2 cup red or white wine
8 large white potatoes	salt/pepper
(cut in quarters)	

Heat olive oil in 6 qt. pot, add beef, salt, pepper and oregano. Brown well. Add tomato paste, wine and water to almost cover meat. Mix liquids well until gravy thickens slightly. Simmer 45 minutes. Add potatoes and simmer until fork tender, stirring occasioinally about 15-20 minutes. Serve hot with fresh Italian bread. It's simple but gooooood!

Origin: My father's father taught him to make it, he taught me and I will teach my son.

Bob Borella
Joseph A. Franzalia Lodge #2422

Polpettone Ripieno
(Stuffed Meat Loaf)

1 1/2-2 lbs. ground beef
1/2-1 cup Parmesan cheese
2 garlic cloves, chopped
6 leaves fresh parsley, chopped
Olive oil for frying
salt/pepper

1 1/2 cups bread crumbs
2 eggs, plus 1/2 cup water
  (more water if needed)
1/2 lb. mozzarella
  (cut lengthwise into 4 pieces)

Mix all ingredients thoroughly (except mozzarella pieces) and form into a firmly packed football shape. Make a deep lengthwise slit and stuff with mozzarella; close meat loaf firmly.

Heat oil in a large fry pan and brown meat loaf on all sides. Gently lift out and place in simmering tomato sauce to cook slowly 30-45 minutes on low heat. Serve sliced with pasta or rice.

Origin: Rose Paulantonio Cuccinelli, my mother-in-law.

Edith Cuccinelli
Sgt. F. M. Bonanno Lodge #2549

Variation
2 hard boiled eggs, sliced thin
1/4 lb. salami, sliced thin
1/2 cup Parmesan cheese
1 garlic clove, minced

1/4 cup ham, diced
1 cup mozzarella, shredded
2 tbsp. parsley, chopped

Pat meat ball mixture flat onto a sheet of wax paper to 1" thick. Layer eggs, salami and ham; then sprinkle mozzarella, Parmesan cheese, garlic and parsley evenly over top. Pick up wax paper on long end and start to roll like a jelly roll. Pat firmly into a meatball and seal ends. Follow above directions to complete recipe.

Origin: Sabina D'Alessandro, my mother-in-law

Jeanette D'Alessandro
Coral Springs Lodge #2332

Sicilian Pot Roast

4 lbs. Beef rump roast
2 oz. salt pork, chopped
8 black olives
8 stuffed olives
1 large can plum tomatoes
   (crushed)
Flour for dredging

1 large onion, sliced
salt/pepper
1/4 cup raisins
4 tbsp. Olive oil
1 garlic clove, chopped

Cut slits into meat and stuff alternately with black olives, stuffed olives, bits of garlic and salt pork. Dredge the meat with flour and brown in hot oil. Add tomatoes, raisins and onions; season with salt and pepper. Cover and cook in moderate 350 degree oven 2 1/2 hours or until tender. Check occasionally, and add water if needed.

Al Gritte
John Paul I Lodge #2427

Braciole ✻

1 lb. top round steak
1/3 cup Parmesan cheese
2 garlic cloves, chopped or
   (garlic powder)
1/4 cup raisins

4-6 mozzarella slices
4-6 tsp. butter
salt/pepper
Olive oil

Cut steak into 4-6 pieces and pound each piece to flatten very thin. Place mozzarella and butter on each piece then sprinkle with Parmesan, garlic, salt and pepper. Roll each piece and tie securely with string.

Saute in olive oil with salt and pepper until steak rolls are browned on all sides. Drop into your favorite tomato sauce and simmer 1 1/2 hours or until fork tender. Remove from sauce, let cool slightly then carefully remove string and serve with your favorite pasta.

Origin: Grace DeLorenzo Croce, my mother-in-law Naples, Italy.

Shirley C. DeLorenzo
Joseph A. Franzalia Lodge #2422

Variation: Add to the above ingredients -

1/4 cup pignoli nuts
4 tbsp. parsley, chopped

Rose Migliorelli
John Paul I Lodge #2427

Braciolone
(Stuffed Rolled Beef)

1 lb. top round steak	1 medium onion, sliced
(sliced thin)	4 tbsp. parsley, chopped
4 tbsp. butter	salt/pepper
1/4 cup Parmesan cheese	Olive oil
1/4 cup bread crumbs	1 cup red wine
2 garlic cloves, chopped	

Spread steak with butter and layer onions over top. Sprinkle remaining ingredients. Roll up tightly and tie securely. Brown in olive oil, turning often so as not to burn. Lower heat, add wine, cover and cook slowly until fork tender, about 1 hour. Braciolone may also be cooked in tomato sauce.

Flo Carbone
Sunrise-Tamarac Lodge #2542

Variation

2 tbsp. grated cheese	1 egg
1 tbsp. parsley, chopped	1 cup mozzarella, grated
2 tsp. oregano	1 tbsp. onion, chopped
1/2 cup wine	1 cup tomato sauce

Spread steak with the above ingredients, roll meat tightly and tie with string. Place in a shallow baking dish. Combine 1 cup of tomato sauce with 1/2 cup wine and pour over top. Bake 350 degrees for an hour or until tender.

Chris Palmer
John Paul I Lodge #2427

Variation

1/2 lb. ground beef	4 bacon strips
1/4 cup bread crumbs	1/2 bunch scallions, chopped
1 egg, beaten	1 tsp. basil
4 tbsp. Parmesan cheese	4 tbsp. parsley, chopped
4 tbsp. raisins	1 garlic clove, chopped
2 eggs. hard boiled	tomato sauce

Place steak flat, layer strips of bacon over top. Combine the above ingredients and layer over bacon. Place hard boiled eggs down the center. Roll tightly and secure with string. Brown well on all sides and gently pour your favorite tomato sauce over meat. Cook slowly 1 hour. Serve sliced with your favorite pasta.

Mary Pullara
La Nuova Sicilia Lodge #1251

Costata alla Pizzaiola
(Steak in Tomato Sauce)

2 lbs. Delmonico or shell steak
1 tbsp. olive oil
2 garlic cloves, minced
1 tbsp. butter

1/4 tsp. oregano
2 tbsp. parsley, chopped
salt/pepper
3/4 cup tomatoes, peeled/chopped

Trim fat from steak. Heat oil in a skillet and brown the steak over high heat 3 minutes on each side. Remove from pan and keep hot. Add garlic, butter, tomatoes and oregano to the skillet. Cook over medium heat, 10 minutes. Return the steak and cook over low heat for 5 minutes or desired degree of rareness. Sprinkle with parsley, salt and pepper. Serves 3-4.

Origin: One of my father's recipe

Anthony Simeone
John Paul I Lodge #2427

Steak alla Salmoriglio

2 Delmonico steaks
4 garlic cloves, minced
2 tbsp. parsley, chopped
2 cups water

2 tblsp. olive oil
1/2 tsp. oregano
salt/pepper
garlic powder

Salmoriglio: Combine water, garlic, parsley 1/4 tsp oregano, salt, pepper and olive oil in a small sauce pan. Boil for 5 minutes and set aside.

Season steaks with salt, pepper, garlic powder and 1/4 tsp. oregano. Place steaks on a grooved broiler pan, so as to catch steak drippings. Broil 3-4 minutes on each side to medium rare. Serve steak in a deep dish with drippings. Pour Salmoriglio sauce over steak. Serve hot with lots of crusty bread to dip into the delicious *"Sammurigghiu"*.

Origin: My mother Maria Inzano, San Pier Niceto, Sicily

Ann Borgia
Sgt. F. M. Bonanno Lodge #2549

Meat Loaf
(Beef and Sausage)

1 lb. lean ground beef
1 medium can tomatoes, (crushed)
1/2 cup onion, chopped
1 egg, beaten

1/2 lb. sausage, (remove casing)
1 cup fresh bread crumbs
1/2 cup bell pepper, chopped
salt/pepper

Combine all ingredients; mix well. Place in 4 1/2" x 8" loaf pan. Bake at 350 degrees 1 hour. Serves 6.

"Bono Appetito Y'ALL"

Ann Varalla
Joseph A. Franzalia Lodge #2422

Marino's Italian Barbecue
(Beef and Sausage)

5 lbs. Sweet Italian sausage
  (remove casing)
3 lbs. round steak, chopped
6 large green peppers
  (sliced)
8 fresh plum tomatoes
  (cut in quarters)

2 1/2 lbs. Hot Italian sausage
  (remove casing)
2 extra large Bermuda onions
  (sliced)
garlic powder
salt/pepper
1/4 tsp. oregano

Combine the ingredients in a very large fry pan. I use a 17" camping fry pan. Season generously with garlic powder, salt, pepper and oregano. Cook over hot coals. Stir and mix often to prevent sticking. Let all the juices cook out and evaporate. According to the fire, it should take approximately 1 hour. Spoon the barbecue mixture onto rolls and enjoy. All the vegetables will dissolve and you will have a mixture of cooked chopped meats. Quantity for large group of 25 for lunch, snack or first course.

Old family recipe for large family gatherings. We always looked forward to the summer months and our family barbecues.

Origin: DeJon, Salerno

Gladys Marino
Sunrise-Tamarac Lodge #2542

Sausage Pastiera

8 oz. egg pastina
6 cups boiling water
salt/pepper
1/2 cup Parmesan cheese

6 oz. Italian sweet sausage
(semi-dried or fresh)*
4 eggs, beaten

Preheat oven 350 degrees. Oil a 9" pie pan. Cook pastene in boiling water for 5 minutes, drain well.

Cut sausage lengthwise, slice 1/4" thick or if using fresh sausage, remove casing and crumble. In a large bowl add eggs, sausage, pastene, Parmesan cheese and pepper. Pour mixture into pie plate. Bake 1 hour or until knife inserted in center comes out clean. Let stand 5 minutes before cutting. Serves 8.

Great accompaniment to soup or served with salad for a luncheon dish.

*Note: To dry Italian sausage, place links on refrigerator shelf, turn over each day. Sausage will lose its moisture in about 4 days.

Grayce DeBartolo
Sgt. F. M. Bonanno Lodge #2549

Sausage and Peppers ☆

1 lb. sausage, uncut
2 medium peppers, sliced
2 tbsp. red wine

2 medium onions, sliced
3 tbsp. olive oil

Saute peppers and onions in olive oil until wilted. Remove. Add sausage to fry pan in coil shape. Cook slowly to brown. Flip over to cook other side. When browned, cut sausage into pieces, add wine, peppers and onions over top of sausage. Continue to cook until sausage is no longer pink and peppers and onions are soft.

Grace Campisi
La Nuova Sicilia Lodge #1251

Fegato alla Veneziana
(Calves Liver Veneziano)

1 1/2 lbs. calves liver (sliced, 1" thick)	1/4 cup flour
	salt/pepper
1/4 cup butter or margarine	1/4 cup olive oil
2 lbs. onions, sliced thin	1/2 tsp. dried sage leaves
1/4 cup dry white wine	1 tbsp. lemon juice
2 tbsp. parsley, chopped	

Chill liver in freezer 15-20 minutes; then slice in narrow strips 2-3" long. Roll liver into flour, salt and pepper coating well.

Heat butter and 2 tablespoons of oil, saute liver strips, until browned. about 5 minutes. Remove and set aside. Add remaining oil to skillet, saute onions stirring until golden brown about 10 minutes. Add sage and liver; cook covered over low heat 5 minutes.

Remove liver and onion to serving dish. To drippings in skillet, add wine and lemon juice, bring to a boil and stir. Pour over liver and onions. Sprinkle with chopped parsley. Serves 6-8.

Origin: My mother's recipe Alberta Di Corte

Laura D. Spoto
La Nuova Sicilia Lodge #1251

Fegatelli di Maiale con La Rete
(Pork Liver Wrapped in Caul Fat)

1 1/2 lbs. pork liver	salt
1 lb. Caul fat	coarse ground pepper
bay leaves	

Soak caul fat in warm water for 5 minutes until it becomes soft. Cut membrane into pieces about 5" x 7" and cut liver 1" thick, 2" wide and 3" long. Season each piece with salt and grinding of black pepper. Place a bay leaf on each piece of liver and wrap with caul fat. Secure with a toothpick.

Liver bundles may be grilled on a barbecue or broiled in the oven 2-3 minutes on each side. My father sauteed the liver in a heavy fry pan and let the caul fat self baste the liver. *Do not overcook, the liver should be pink and juicy.* Serve hot.

"Caul fat" or "Pork Net" may be ordered from your butcher.

Origin: My father, Raul Giuliani - Mondolfo, Italy

Rose Marie Boniello
Sgt. F. M. Bonanno Lodge #2549

Fegato "Garbo e Dolce"
(Sweet and Sour Liver)

1 lb. calves liver (sliced thin)
1 egg
1/2 tsp. salt
1/4 cup flour

1/2 cup bread crumbs
1/2 cup butter
1 tbsp. lemon juice
3/4 tsp. sugar

Beat egg with salt. Lightly flour liver and dip into beaten egg and then bread crumbs. Heat the butter in a fry pan and quickly fry until lightly browned. Place on a heated serving dish and keep warm.

In same fry pan, slowly heat lemon juice with sugar, stir until sugar is dissolved. Pour over liver, serve hot. Serves 4.

Anthony Simeone
John Paul I Lodge #2427

Pork and Vinegar Peppers

6-7 lbs. fresh pork shoulder
1 very large onion, sliced
3 large baking potatoes
   (cut in pieces)

1 large jar vinegar peppers
   (sliced, reserve vinegar)
salt/pepper
garlic powder
white vinegar

Bone the pork shoulder, trim fat and skin and cut into 1" cubes. (The bone and skin can be used in a tomato sauce.)

Place meat in a roasting pan, season with salt, pepper and garlic . Cook at 350 degrees for 1 hour. Remove from oven and drain. Add potatoes and peppers. Combine reserved vinegar with equal parts of white vinegar and water to make 1 cup. Add to pan and cover with foil and bake 1/2 hour. Remove from oven, uncover, stir and bake an additional 1/2 hour.

Years ago when the family met Sunday outdoors at the grandparents' home, this was cooked in a large homemade outdoor oven similar to a pizza oven.

Origin: Marino family - from De Jon, Salerno

Gladys Marino
Sunrise-Tamarac Lodge #2542

Panini di Fette di Maiale Inpanati
(Breaded Center Pork Loin Sandwiches)

1 lb. center cut pork loin	1/2 cup olive oil
2 eggs, beaten	1/2 cup Marinara sauce
1 cup seasoned bread crumbs	1 loaf Italian bread

Trim fat from pok and cut into 8 slices. Pound each slice to 1/8" thickness. Dip into egg, then bread crumbs on both sides. Fry cutlets in hot oil until golden brown. Place meat on slices of bread, top with 1-2 tbsp. Marinara sauce. Makes 8 sandwiches.

Angelo Tacchi
Port St. Lucie Lodge #2594

Porchetta
(Roasted Whole Pig)

40-50 lb. whole pig, split (head removed)	15 oz. jar whole fennel seeds
1 box salt	3 lb. jar fresh garlic cloves (or 12 whole garlic heads)
16 oz. jar coarse ground pepper	grill, 2 X 4 with a hood
	20 lbs. charcoal

Before pig is placed on the grill, make slits in the skin 4" apart. Stuff each pocket with a garlic clove, fennel seeds, salt and pepper. Then salt and pepper the entire pig generously.

It takes 1/2 hour for charcoal briquettes to get hot enough to have a gray ash. Place pig skin side down on the grill. Brush marinate generously on the inside cavity. Pierce meat with a knife to form pockets and insert garlic, fennel seeds, salt and pepper. Close hood and cook for 1 hour.

Turn pig, marinate skin side, close hood and roast 1 1/2 hours. Turn pig every hour, marinating generously each time. *It takes about 5 hours to cook.*

Marinate: Bring to a boil and simmer for 5 minutes, 2 qts. of water, 10 oz. whole fennel seeds, 2 cups olive oil, 1 cup chopped garlic, 4 tbsp. salt, 1/3 cup coarse black pepper.

Comments: To prevent smoke, I use a 2 X 4 aluminum sheet to cover my grill. This keeps the fat from dripping on the coals. I keep the grill tipped slightly to allow the fat to run off into a bucket.

John Boniello
Sgt. F. M. Bonanno Lodge #2549

Pork Roast Calabrese ⭐

4-5 lbs. loin of pork, boneless	2 garlic cloves
2 tbsp. rosemary	2 tbsp. parsley, chopped
1/4 lb. fontina or swiss cheese	1/4 lb. prosciutto
(cut in 2-3" strips)	(cut in 2-3" strips)
1/4 lb. salami, 1/4" pieces	1/3 cup olive oil
salt/pepper	anchovies (optional)

Prepare pork loin to be stuffed by cutting 2 lenthwise slits along the side. Rub meat with garlic and sprinkle rosemary into slits. Stuff each opening with cheese, prosciutto, salami and capers. Tie meat with string to encase stuffing. Season loin with salt, pepper and rosemary, place in a roasting pan and pour olive oil over top.

Roast in a preheated oven 450 degrees for 20 minutes. Lower temperature to 350 degrees and roast for 1 1/4 hours, turning occasionally. Remove from oven and let stand 15 minutes before slicing. Serve hot or at room temperature. Serves 6.

Origin: From grandparents - Maida, Calabria

Tom Bevino
Joseph A. Franzalia Lodge #2422

Roast Leg of Lamb with Artichokes

4-5 lb. leg of lamb	2-3 garlic cloves, slivered
juice of 1 lemon	2 tsp. salt
1 tsp. pepper	1 tsp. oregano
6 small or 3 large artichokes	2 cups tomato sauce
(fresh)	1 cup water
1 lemon, sliced	

Make slits with tip of knife in several places around leg of lamb. Insert garlic slivers into each slit. Rub lamb with lemon juice, salt, pepper and oregano. Place in a shallow baking pan and roast at 400 degrees for 30 minutes. Reduce heat to 350 degrees, baste with drippings and continue roasting 1 hour, skim off excess fat. Trim artichoke stems, leaving 1/2" stubs. Snip off tips and remove chokes. Cut large artichokes in half. Add tomato sauce and water to roasting pan. Arrange artichokes cut-side down in sauce around lamb roast. Cook an additional 1 hour. Total roasting time 2 hours 30 minutes. Serves 4-6. **Buon Appetito!**

Origin: Argento, Sicily my father and mother's home town

Laura Spoto
La Nuova Sicilia Lodge #1251

Lamb Shanks Giardiniera

4 (1 lb.) lamb shanks
2 carrots, diced
1 large can plum tomatoes
   (crushed)
8 oz. Fettuccine
garlic powder

2 medium onions, diced
1 can peas with liquid
4 oz. red or white dry wine
3 basil leaves
salt/pepper
rosemary leaves

Trim all fat from shanks, season with salt, pepper, garlic powder and rosemary leaves. Preheat oil in a heavy pan that will hold shanks comfortably. Brown shanks well on all sides. Add crushed tomatoes, onions, carrots and basil. Simmer for 3 hours, when shanks are tender, add wine and peas. Simmer for a few minutes more while boiling fettuccine. Serve lamb and wine sauce over fettuccine and enjoy this serving for 4.

Philip Borgia
Sgt. F. M. Bonanno Lodge #2549

Baked Lamb Shanks

4 lamb shanks
1 tsp. oregano
1 tsp. salt
1 tbsp. olive oil

1 medium onion, chopped
4 garlic cloves
1 cup white wine
1 tsp. black pepper

Rub lamb with garlic. Make a slit in each shank, insert garlic cloves then season with salt and pepper. Brown in hot olive oil on all sides, in a dutch oven. Remove from pot and set aside. Saute onions with oregano stirring for 5 minutes. Return lamb to pot, pour wine over top, cover and bake at 350 degrees for 2 hours. Serve with rice.

Rose Marie Tufarella
Sunrise-Tamarac Lodge #2542

Roast Leg of Lamb

8 lb. leg of lamb	12 strips bacon or pancetta
6 garlic cloves	whole cloves
mint leaves	salt/pepper
1 onion, sliced	

Make pockets in leg of lamb. Insert small pieces of bacon, garlic and mint leaves. Place lamb in roasting pan; lay 3 strips of bacon and sliced onion over top, brown in hot oven 400 degrees for 30 minutes. Baste frequently until lamb is golden brown. Lower temperature to 325 degrees and roast additional 1 1/2 hours or until tender.

Leg of lamb is an Easter tradition in my family. My parents prepared the fresh lamb a day or two before Easter. Serves 6-8.

Origin: Avellino and Potenza, Provence Di Basilicata.

Ellen C. Feigenbaum
Ft. Lauderdale Lodge #2263

Spezzatini Di Agnello con Piselli
(Lamb Stew with Peas)

2 lbs. boneless lamb for stew	1/4 cup flour
3-4 tbsp. olive oil	1 garlic clove, minced
salt/pepper	1 tbsp. parsley, minced
1 cup dry white wine	2 cups whole tomatoes, crushed
2 cups peas, or	6 eggs
(10 oz. pkg. frozen peas)	1/2 cup Parmesan cheese

Dredge bite size pieces of lamb in flour. Heat olive oil, saute garlic, lamb, salt, pepper and brown slowly. Add parsley, wine, tomatoes and a little water to cover the lamb. Cover pot and simmer on low for about 45 minutes. *Stir often, add water as needed.*

When meat is tender, add peas and cook 5-10 minutes longer. Beat eggs with grated cheese and pour over lamb. Stir gently until eggs are slightly cooked. Remove from heat. The eggs will continue to cook.

Our family serves this stew in small portions as a soup course for Easter dinner.

Origin: My mother-in-law Rosina Boniello

Rose Marie Boniello
Sgt. F. M. Bonanno Lodge # 2549

Roasted Lamb with Pesto

6 lbs. boneless leg of lamb
   (butterfly)
1 cup fresh mint
1/3 cup pignoli nuts
2 garlic cloves
1/2 tsp. coarse ground pepper

1 1/2 cups red wine
1 1/2 cups chicken broth
1/2 cups bread crumbs
2 tbsp. olive oil
1 tsp. salt

Mint Pesto: Combine mint, bread crumbs, pignoli nuts, oil, garlic, salt and pepper in food processor. Process with several on/off motions.

Place lamb, fat side down. Spread mint pesto over meat. Roll lamb from short end and tie with kitchen string. Be sure lamb is at room temperature before roasting begins.

Preheat oven to 450 degrees, roast 30 minutes. Reduce heat to 350 degrees and continue roasting for 50 minutes. Meat thermometer should read 150 for medium rare. Place lamb on warmed serving platter and let rest for 10 minutes before slicing. Add wine and broth to roasting pan, boil slowly, scraping up brown bits. Reduce to 2 cups. Degrease and serve with sliced lamb.

Rosalene Boniello Feller
Submitted by John Boniello
Sgt. F. M. Bonanno Lodge #2549

Grilled Leg of Lamb

5-7 lbs. leg of lamb, boned
   (pounded to even thickness)
1 cup olive oil
1 cup dry white wine
1 tsp. thyme
1 tsp. oregano

salt/pepper
1/2 tsp. rosemary
2 garlic cloves, minced
2 tsp. mint leaves, chopped
2 tsp. fresh basil
2 tbsp. fresh lemon juice

Place lamb in a non-metal pan to marinate. Mix all ingredients and pour over lamb. Turn meat over in marinade. Cover and refrigerate overnight. Turn in morning.

Drain lamb and reserve marinade. Grill 6" from coals for 30 minutes, basting with marinade every 10 minutes. I like lamb pink but cook longer if you prefer well-done. Cut into thin slices and sprinkle with additional finely chopped mint to garnish.

Alfred Zucaro, Jr.
Justin Antonin Scalia Lodge #2235

PESCE/
FISH

Baked Fish Fillet

2-3 lbs. fillet of fish   1/4 lb. margarine
lemon juice   salt/pepper
dry white wine   Parmesan cheese
paprika

Salt and pepper fillets of fish. Put margarine in shallow baking dish in hot oven 400-500 degrees, until browned. The browned margarine gives the distinctive flavor. Place fillets in hot margarine and return to oven 10-15 minutes. Turn fish over and baste with juice. Sprinkle each piece with lemon juice, wine, Parmesan cheese and paprika. Baste, return to oven approximately 5 minutes.

Gloria (Scalzitti) Walker
Joseph A. Franzalia Lodge #2422

Pesce al Forno con Patate
(Baked Fish with Potatoes)

3-4 lbs. filet of fish (Red Snapper) 2 large onions, chopped
1 green pepper, chopped   4 celery stalks, chopped
2-3 garlic cloves, chopped   1/2 bunch parsley, chopped
2-3 bay leaves   pinch of sugar
1 can stewed tomatoes (blended   4-6 potatoes, cut-up
   in processor or blender)   olive oil

Saute onions, pepper, celery, garlic and parsley in olive oil. Add blended tomatoes and bay leaves. Cook approximately for 1 hour, add sugar. Oil a roasting pan, season the fish with salt and pepper. Place fish in pan with cut-up potatoes. Pour sauce over potatoes and fish. Bake for approximately 1 hour. Basting every 15 minutes. Serves 6-8

Mary Palori
La Nuova Sicilia Lodge #1251

Mussels and Shrimp with Penne

1 tbsp. olive oil
1/8 tsp. crushed red pepper flakes
  (optional)
2 tbsp. parsley, finely chopped
1 tsp. mint leaf, crumbled
3/4 lb. med. shrimp
  (shell/devein)
1 tbsp. brandy, optional
2 tbsp. parsley, chopped fine

2-3 garlic cloves, chopped fine
2 cups fresh tomatoes
  (chopped, peeled, seeded)
1 tsp. leaf basil, crumbled
1/4 cup bottled clam juice
1 lb. mussels in shells
  (scrubbed, beards removed)
1 lb. Penne
1 lemon rind, grated

Saute garlic and pepper flakes in olive oil, until garlic just begins to color, 2-3 minutes. Add tomatoes, parsley, basil and mint bring to boil - lower heat, cover and simmer 10 minutes. Add clam juice and shrimp, cover; cook over low heat 2 minutes stirring once. Add mussels and brandy, cover and cook for 2-3 minutes longer or until shrimp are pink and mussels open. Carefully remove mussels from sauce. Cook pasta al dente, drain and place in warm serving bowl, top pasta with hot sauce, stir to mix well. Place mussels on top. Garnish with chopped parsley and lemon rind. *It's Delicious, It's Light ..... It's Italian.*

Ellen C. Feigenbaum
Fort Lauderdale Lodge #2263

Shrimp Primavera

3 tomatoes, peeled and chopped
1/2 cup water
1/4 cup onion, chopped
2 tbsp. snipped fresh basil
  (or dried basil, crushed)
dash pepper
1 lb. fresh or frozen shrimp
  (cook/shell)
1/3 cup grated Parmesan cheese

1 cup mushrooms, sliced
1/3 cup tomato paste
1/4 cup snipped parsley
1 tsp. sugar
1/4 tsp. salt
1 garlic clove, minced
1 lb. fresh asparagus
12 oz. hot cooked fettuccine

In medium saucepan combine tomatoes, mushrooms, water, tomato paste, onion, parsley, basil, sugar, salt, pepper and garlic. Boil gently, uncovered about 20 minutes, stirring occasionally. Add the shrimp, heat through.

Meanwhile, cook the asparagus, covered, in small amount of boiling water about 3 minutes, drain. Arrange fettuccine, shrimp mixture and asparagus on plates. Sprinkle with Parmesan cheese. Serves 6. **Buon Appetito!**

Laura Spoto
La Nuova Sicilia Lodge #1251

Gamberi al Forno
(Baked Shrimp)

12 jumbo shrimp
2 eggs, beaten
1/2 cup parlsey, chopped

2 cups flavored bread crumbs
5 garlic cloves, chopped
1/2 cup olive oil

Peel and devein shrimp, dip in egg then roll in bread crumbs and place in a lightly oiled shallow baking dish. Sprinkle garlic and parsley over top. Pour oil over shrimp. Heat oven to 400 degrees, bake for 20 minutes or until cooked. *(Do not overcook.)*

Edythe Dell'Orfono
Sunrise-Tamarac Lodge #2542

Calamari Fritti
(Fried Squid)

3 lbs. squid, cleaned
2 eggs
1 tbsp. grated onion
salt/pepper

1 cup flour
1 12 oz. can beer
1 garlic clove, minced
olive oil

Cut squid in 1" rings. Combine flour, eggs, beer, onion, garlic, salt and pepper. Dip small handful of squid rings in flour and egg batter. Deep fry in hot oil until brown and tender. Remove with slotted spoon and drain on paper towel. Garnish with lemon slices.

Rings may be dipped in a Marinara sauce or Cocktail sauce.

Frances Tomasulo
John Paul I Lodge #2427

Variation:

Clean squid, cut in pieces
1 tbsp. milk
salt/pepper

1 large egg, beaten
3/4 cup fine bread crumbs
olive oil

Dip squid pieces in combined egg and milk. Roll into bread crumbs. Let coated squid stand while oil heats. Fry 8-10 pieces at a time until light brown. Remove with a slotted spoon to paper towel, let drain.

Rose Marie Tufarella
Sunrise-Tamarac Lodge #2542

Calamari Ripieni
(Stuffed Squid)

1 1/2 lbs. squid (calamari)	3 tbsp. olive oil
4 garlic cloves, chopped	2 tbsp. onion, chopped
2 sprigs of parsley	1/2 cup bread crumbs
2 tbsp. celery, chopped	salt/pepper
Marinara sauce	

Skin squid and remove insides and wash thoroughly. Keeping body whole. Remove tentacles and eyes.

Saute garlic, celery, onion in olive oil, add parsley and bread crumbs. Mix well and stuff the squid with a teaspoon. Close with tooth picks. Saute stuffed squid on both sides for about 10 minutes. Add Marinara sauce and simmer 25-30 minutes, until squid is tender. Remove cooked squid (calamari) pour sauce over pasta, serve calamari on side.

Esther Messina
John Paul I Lodge #2427

Variation:

Omit onion and celery. Retain tentacles and clean. Add 4 tablespoons grating cheese to bread crumbs and moistened with water and oil, add 1 egg to bind bread crumbs. Stuff calamari half full, close with tooth picks. Saute retained tentacles in olive oil and add to Marinara sauce with 2 bay leaves. Add calamari to sauce and simmer 25-30 minutes until fork tender. Remove bay leaves before serving sauce and stuffed calamari over linguine.

Jeanette D'Alessandro
Coral Springs Lodge #2332

Stuffed Calamari

2 lbs. med. size squid, cleaned	2 tbsp. melted butter
1 15 oz. container Ricotta	2 slices white bread, shredded
1/4 cup Parmesan cheese	1 tbsp. parsley
2 eggs	salt/pepper
1/2 cup olive oil	1/8 tsp. oregano powder
2 cups Marinara Sauce	garlic powder

Preheat oven 350 degrees. Wash squid thoroughly and drain well. Combine ricotta with bread, cheese, parsley, eggs, butter, oregano, garlic powder, salt and pepper, mix and blend well. Stuff squid with mixture and sew or fasten opening with toothpicks. Brown quickly in hot olive oil until squid turns slightly pink. Take squid out of pan with slotted spoon and place in a deep baking dish. Pour tomato sauce over squid. Bake until tender, about 45 minutes. Serves 2-4

Rose Marie Tufarella
Sunrise-Tamarac Lodge #2542

Calamari Adriatica
(Squid Adriatic)

2 lbs. fresh or frozen squid
3/4 cup olive oil
1 onion or scallions, chopped
1 garlic clove, minced

1 tsp. fresh or dried basil
1 sprig parsley, chopped
1/2 cup red wine
16 oz. can tomatoes, crushed

Remove inside and skin from squid, wash thoroughly. Cut into 1/2" rings or pieces about 1" square. Saute squid in hot oil for 1 minute, add parsley, onions, garlic and basil cook for about 5 minutes. Add wine, cover and simmer for 5 more minutes.

Add tomatoes and cook for 1/2 hour or until squid is tender. Add more water as needed, while cooking.

Origin: Abruzzi - 'Ricciardelli' Family

Virginia A. Papale
Sunrise-Tamarac Lodge #2542

Stockfish Messina Style (Sicilian)

1 1/2 lbs. dried stockfish
1/2 cup olive oil
1 medium onion, sliced
1 large can peeled tomatoes
1 1/2 tbsp. pine nuts
1 1/2 tbsp. seedless raisins

2 tbsp. capers
12 black olives, pitted & diced
2-4 potatoes, sliced thin
1/4 tsp. salt
3/4 tsp. pepper
1 cup dry white wine

Soak dried stockfish for 4 days, change water every 6 hours. (Most stockfish and baccala can be purchased presoaked these days.)

Saute onions in olive oil, lightly. Add crushed tomatoes and cook slightly, add pine nuts, raisins, capers, olives, wine and season with salt and pepper. Bring to a low simmer for just a few minutes.

Prepare an oven pan that will take all the above ingredients easily. Cut fish into serving pieces and place into pan, arrange sliced potatoes around fish. Pour tomato sauce over fish and potatoes. Bake in oven 375 degrees for 1 hour or until potatoes are tender and fish flakes easily. Serve with crusty Italian bread and salad.

Esther M. Messina
John Paul I Lodge #2427

Baccala alla Marinara
(Cod Fish Marinara)

2 lbs. Cod steaks, 1" thick
1/2 med. onion, chopped
1/4 cup green olives
   (pitted and chopped)
salt/pepper

2 tbsp. oil
2 cups canned tomatoes, crushed
2 tbsp. capers
1 tbsp. parsley
1/2 tsp. oregano

Oil 1 1/2 quart casserole, place Cod and set aside. Saute onion in olive oil for 2 minutes, add tomatoes, chopped green olives, capers, parsley, salt, pepper and oregano. Bring to boil then pour over Cod. Bake at 350 degrees for 25-30 minutes or until fish flakes when pierced with fork and is tender.

Note: This recipe may be cooked on the top of stove in dutch oven.

Margaret Scarfia
John Paul I Lodge #2427
Grace S. Monte
LaNuova Sicila Lodge #2015

Swordfish alla Messina

2 lbs. swordfish, cut in pieces
   (or black fin shark)
4-6 tbsp. olive oil
1 medium onion, sliced
2 garlic cloves, diced
2 large celery stalks sliced
1 16 oz. can crushed tomatoes
3 tbsp. capers

12 black olives, cut up
12 green olives, cut up
   (or Spanish olives w/pimientos)
2 tbsp. tomato paste
1/2 tsp. oregano
salt/pepper

1 lb. Linguine

Saute onion, garlic, celery in olive oil until onion wilts. Add tomatoes, capers, olives, paste, oregano, salt and pepper. Simmer gently until oil separates, about 15-20 minutes.

Gently lay fish on sauce, poach it until it just flakes about 10 minutes. Remove fish to serving platter, pour sauce over cooked Linguine, serve with crusty bread and salad. *"A Family Favorite"*

Origin: My friend, Sina Henry, Cape Coral, Florida

Rose Marie Boniello
Sgt. F. M. Bonanno Lodge #2549

Merluzzo (Baccala) alla Marchigiana

1 1/2 lb. baccala, soaked	16 oz. crushed tomatoes
4 garlic cloves, diced	4 tbsp. broad leaf parsley
olive oil	(chopped fine)
salt/pepper	flour

Cut baccala into serving pieces, wipe dry and dredge into flour seasoned with salt and pepper. Fry in olive oil until golden brown on each side, until fish flakes. Place on brown paper to drain excess oil. Serve with tomato sauce.

Tomato sauce:

Saute garlic in 4-6 tbsp. olive oil, add crushed tomatoes, parsley, salt and pepper. Let simmer about 20-25 minutes.

Rose Marie Boniello
Sgt. F. M. Bonanno Lodge #2549

Brodetto all' Anconetana
(Soup with Clams and Mussels)

1 1/2 lb. firm white fish	2 doz. mussels, scrubbed
(cut into serving pieces)	(beards removed)
2 doz. small clams, scrubbed	1 lb. cleaned calamari
3-4 tbsp. olive oil	(cut 1" circles, save tentacles)
3-4 garlic cloves, diced	1 can crushed tomatoes
2 tbsp. tomato paste	4-6 tbsp. mint, chopped

In a large dutch oven that will hold all the fish, saute garlic lightly in heated oil. Add crushed tomatoes, salt, pepper, mint and tomato paste. Let cook about 20 minutes. Add mussels, clams, calamari circles and tentacles, let simmer gently 5-10 minutes until shell fish opens and calamari are tender. Add white fish gently on top and continue to simmer about 5-8 minutes until fish flakes. Serve with lots of crusty bread to "dunk" in broth.

Origin: Family Recipe/ Mondolfo, Italy

Rose Marie Boniello
Sgt. F. M. Bonanno Lodge #2549

Fried Smelts alla Anna
(Vinegar and Onion Sauce)

1 lb. Smelts	4 medium onions, sliced
3 tbsp. olive oil	2/3 cup flour
3 tbsp. red wine vinegar	1 egg, beaten
salt/pepper	garlic powder

Clean and trim fins from smelts. Wash with cold water, pat dry on paper towel. Combine flour with salt, pepper and garlic powder. Dip smelts into beaten egg, then roll into seasoned flour. Fry smelts in hot oil until golden brown and place in a glass casserole.

Drain all but 2 tablespoons of oil from skillet. Saute onion in same pan until soft and wilted. Add vinegar; lower heat, cover and steam for 1-2 minutes. Pour onion and vinegar over smelts and cover. Serve at room temperature.

Ann Borgia
Sgt. F. M. Bonanno Lodge #2549

Variation: (Mint and Garlic Sauce)

2 garlic cloves, chopped	1 tbsp. sugar
1/4 cup olive oil	1/4 cup water
1/2 cup wine vinegar	6 fresh mint leaves, chopped

Saute garlic in olive oil to a light color. Remove from heat. Mix vinegar, water, sugar and mint leaves; add to oil and garlic. Return to heat, bring to a boil immediately cover and remove from stove. Let cool, pour over smelts. Serve at room temperature.

Antonette Zaffarano
Sgt. F. M. Bonanno Lodge #2549

Cioppino
(Seafood Stew)

1 1/2 lbs. boned bass, halibut
or grouper
1 lb. shrimp, cleaned and shelled
2 doz. black mussels
(beard removed and scrubbed)
1 cup parsley, chopped
1/2 cup olive oil
6 oz. can tomato paste
1 small lemon, sliced thin
1 tsp. oregano
fresh ground black pepper

3 1/2 lbs. lobster tails
(cut up)
1 doz. small clams, scrubbed
2 cups onion, chopped
1/2 cup green pepper, chopped
6-8 garlic cloves, minced
1 (35 oz.) can plum tomatoes
2 cups dry red wine
1 tsp. basil
salt, optional

Combine onion, green pepper and garlic with the olive oil in a large pot or kettle (similar to pasta pot). Saute over low heat, stirring occasionally about 10 minutes. Add tomatoes, paste, wine, lemon and 1/2 cup of parsley and all the other seasonings. Bring to a boil, reduce heat, cover and simmer for 20 minutes. Add fish, lobsters and shrimp simmer for 5-10 minutes. Add the mussels and clams, simmer 10 more minutes or until the clams and mussels are open.

Serve the Cioppino in soup bowls, on a slice of Italian bread. Sprinkle with parsley. Serve garlic bread and a robust red wine.

Origin: When I first visited San Francisco 23 years ago I was served Cioppino. We enjoyed the mixture of flavors and the strong overtone of Italian cooking. I asked for the recipe and also received this history - The dish was started some 100 years ago, invented by the many Italian immigrants who came from Italy and fished the Pacific waters, for a living. This is their recipe - a distinctive, pungent Mediterranean mixture of tomatoes, basil, oregano, garlic and red wine. Since that trip 23 years ago I have served this stew as part of our Christmas Eve feasting.

Gladys Marino
Sunrise-Tamarac Lodge #2542

Baccala
(Dried Cod Fish)

3 lbs. baccala	1/4 cup raisins
(dried or presoaked)	1/4 cup pignoli nuts
1 cup olive oil	1 tsp. basil
4 garlic cloves, chopped	1 tsp. oregano
1 cup black olives	salt/pepper
1 capers (small jar)	2 lbs. plum tomatoes, chopped

Soak dried baccala in the refrigerator for 3 days. Changing water 3 times a day. (Baccala can now be purchased presoaked.)

Boil black olives for 2 minutes, drain; set aside. Run water over capers, drain; set aside. Place fish in baking pan in a single layer, sprinkle all ingredients over top. Bake 375 degrees for 1 hour.

Our family serves this on Christmas Eve as part of our holiday fish feast.

Rose Testagrosso
Submitted by Gladys Marino
Sunrise-Tamarac Lodge #2542

Variation
Lay celery stalks on the bottom of a large sauce pan. Layer presoaked cod fillets on celery. Then sprinkle with salt, pepper, parsley and bread crumbs. Drizzle olive oil over top. Repeat another layer. Pour 1 cup chicken broth or water over top. Cover and let simmer 1 1/2 hours.

Traditional to my family on Christmas Eve.

Mary A. Sorci
John Paul I Lodge #2427

Calamari Ripieni
(Stuffed Squid)

3 lbs. squid, cleaned	1 cup rice, cooked
2 onions, sliced	4 garlic cloves
1/2 lb. bacon or pancetta	1 egg, beaten
1/4 cup bread crumbs, seasoned	2-3 cups Marinara sauce
4 tbsp. olive oil	1/2 tsp. oregano
1/4 tsp. red pepper flakes	

Filling
Saute onion and garlic until golden brown. Add oregano and red pepper, set aside. Cook bacon until crisp, drain and set aside.

continued on next page

Calamari Ripieni
(Stuffed Squid)
continued

Mix rice, onion, garlic, bacon and egg. Add bread crumbs to blend the filling. Fill each squid with stuffing, close top with a toothpick and layer in a baking dish. Cover with Marinara sauce and bake in a preheated oven 350 degrees for 1/2 hour.

Enjoyed by our family as part of our Christmas Eve fish feast.

Rose Testagrossa
Submitted by Gladys Marino
Sunrise-Tamarac Lodge #2542

Zuppa di Baccala
(Cod Fish Soup)

5 tbsp. olive oil
1 medium onion, sliced
5 large ribs of celery
  (with leaves)
3/4 cup tomato puree or
  (4 tbsp. tomato paste)
2 large heads escarole

1 whole cauliflower
1/4 cup pignoli nuts
6 dried figs, cut in pieces
1/2 cup dark raisins
1 lb. piece dried baccala
salt/pepper

Soak baccala in water for 2 days, covered in the refrigerator. Change water 3 times a day. (You can now buy presoaked baccala.)

Cut celery and leaves into 1" pieces, set aside. Wash escarole, cut into bite size pieces scald and drain. Set aside. (I save tender white leaves for salad.) Cut cauliflower into small flowerets and scald, drain and set aside. In an 8 quart soup pot, saute onion in olive oil, till limp. Add celery, saute for 1-2 minutes, then add tomato puree. Stir to mix well. Remove from heat. Add escarole, cauliflower, pignoli, figs and raisins. Cover vegetables and fruit with water. Add salt and pepper. Stir gently to mix. Cut soaked baccala into 2" pieces, place on top of vegetable mixture. DO NOT STIR. Mix vegetables gently during cooking with a fork. Cover and simmer 25-30 minutes, adding water as needed. Remove baccala to a platter. Serve vegetables and broth in soup bowls. Place pieces of baccala on top.

In my family, this soup is served for lunch with zeppole on Christmas Eve day.

Origin: Grandma Rosina Boniello

Rose Marie Boniello
Sgt. F. M. Boniello Lodge #2549

Lumache, Bovoloni, Babalu
(Snails)

4 doz. snails
4 garlic cloves, minced
1/4 cup olive oil
1 cup water

2 (28 oz.) can tomato puree
4 tbsp. fresh mint, chopped
salt/pepper

Prepare Snails:

Add 2 tablespoons salt and 1/2 cup vinegar to a large pot of cold water. Add snails, stir until completely covered with foam, drain. Repeat this procedure 3-4 times until there is no more foam. Wash snails under cold running water until free from salt and vinegar. Put them in a pan with cold water to cover and set aside.

Sauce:

Saute garlic lightly in oil, add tomatoes, salt and pepper and let simmer for 10 minutes. Add 1 cup of water and mint leaves; simmer 15 minutes. Sauce should be thin and enough sauce to cover snails. Drain water from snails. Let snails breathe and start to poke heads out of shells. As snails emerge from shells drop into simmering sauce. Stir and simmer slowly for 30 minutes. Add a little water, if needed. Serve snails in their shells with snail pricks or extra large safety pins. Enjoy with lots of fresh baked crusty bread.

Origin: My grandmother Maria Lorenzini

> *I enjoyed eating "Lumache" as a child and still delight in the memory of helping "Nona" capture the snails that escaped from her pot.*

Rose Marie Boniello
Sgt. F. M. Bonanno Lodge #2549

Variation:

1 medium onion, basil, oregano, parsley (omit mint). Saute onion with garlic and add the above spices to the tomato sauce. Serve with side dish of macaroni, crusty bread and a salad.

Mary Sorci
John Paul I Lodge #2427

POLLO/
POULTRY

Chicken and Sausage ✚

6 medium potatoes
 (peeled and quartered)
2 tsp. oregano
1/3 cup Olive oil
1 lb. sausage (sweet/hot)
 (cut into 1" pieces)

1/2 tsp. black pepper
2 tsp. paprika
3 lb. frying chicken
 (cut into serving pieces)
1 tsp. garlic salt

Arrange potatoes in a large shallow baking pan. Mix all of the seasonings together and sprinkle half on the potatoes. Arrange the chicken and sausage pieces on top. Pour the oil over the ingredients and sprinkle with the remaining seasonings. Cover with foil and bake in 425 degree oven for 1/2 hour. Reduce the heat to 375 degrees, uncover, and bake for 45 minutes longer until chicken and sausages are brown. Serves 6.

Jo Lazzaro
Submitted By Edythe Dell'Orfano
Sunrise-Tamarac Lodge #2542

Variation:
Add 3 green peppers sliced, 1 medium onion sliced and 4 tbsp. parsley chopped.

Marie Runfola
Joseph A. Franzalia Lodge #2422

Chicken and Sausage Scarpariello

3 lbs. boneless chicken breasts
3 lbs. hot or sweet sausage
2 lbs. green\red peppers, sliced
2 medium onions, sliced
salt/pepper

1 small bottle sliced hot cherry
 peppers and juice
1/2 tsp. oregano
1/2 cup olive oil

Grill sausage and chicken breasts on a barbeque grill or broil in the oven, until partially cooked. In a large skillet, heat olive oil and saute garlic, onions, green and red peppers, oregano, salt and pepper until partially cooked. Cut sausage and chicken into bite size pieces. Combine meats with peppers and onions. Add hot peppers and juice, stir and continue to cook 10-15 minutes until chicken is fork tender. Serves 8-12.

Origin: Family favorite

Carlo Boniello
Sgt. F. M. Bonanno Lodge #2549

Roast Chicken

4 lb. roasting chicken	2 tsp. oregano
2 garlic cloves, chopped	4 tbsp. butter or olive oil
salt/pepper	1/2 cup red wine vinegar

Cut chicken into serving pieces, wash and dry thoroughly. Butter roasting pan, lay pieces skin side down. Sprinkle with salt, pepper, oregano, parsley and chopped garlic. Put dabs of butter on chicken then sprinkle with vinegar. Bake in a preheated oven 350 degrees for 1 hour.

Origin: Grandma Becce's

Victoria R. Casario
Jerry Barletta Lodge #2502

Variation: OMIT OREGANO
Add five potatoes quartered, 1/2 cup raisins, 1/2 cup romano cheese, grated, 1/2 cup pignoli nuts and 2 tbsp. basil.

Origin: My father

Diane Staffiero Barter
Key West Lodge #2436

Chicken alla Spina

1 whole chicken	salt/pepper
(cut in serving pieces	1 tsp oregano
oil for frying	4 oz. red wine
3 large onions	

Brown chicken in oil, set aside. Lightly saute onions in same oil. Place chicken in a roasting pan. Layer onions over top and sprinkle salt, pepper and oregano. Cover pan, bake 350 degrees 1/2 hour. Add wine and bake additional 1/2 hour, stirring occasionally. Serve with a loaf of Italian bread.

Origin: Regalbuto, Italy

Dora Battaglia
Lake Worth/Boynton Beach Lodge #2304

Petti di Pollo alla Bolognese
(Chicken Breasts with Prosciutto and Cheese)

4 boneless chicken breasts	2 tbsp. oil
1/4 cup flour	8 slices prosciutto
salt/pepper	8 slices Fontina cheese
3 tbsp. butter	or Bel Paese
1/4 cup chicken stock	4 tbsp. Parmesan cheese, grated

Cut chicken breasts in half and pound lightly. Mix flour, salt and pepper. Dredge chicken into seasoned flour. Heat olive oil and butter, add chicken and saute quickly to a golden brown. Place chicken in a buttered baking dish and layer top with prosciutto and cheese slices. Sprinkle grated cheese and chicken stock over all. Bake uncovered for 10 minutes until cheese is melted and lightly browned.

Origin: My mother, Rosa Cellucci

Maria Cellucci Atkins
Key West Lodge #2436

Chicken and Artichokes

6 boneless chicken breasts	3-4 garlic cloves
1 cup bread crumbs, seasoned	salt/pepper
1/2 olive oil	3 tbsp. parsley, chopped
1/4 cup Tarragon vinegar	2 jars artichoke hearts
	(drained/cut in half)

Cut chicken into bite size pieces, and roll in bread crumbs. Heat oil and saute garlic to a golden color and remove. Add chicken, saute to a light brown on both sides. Place chicken in a large baking dish, add sauteed garlic, salt, pepper and vinegar. Sprinkle with parsley. Bake at 350 degrees for 30 minutes. Add artichokes and bake 10 minutes more.

Origin: Grandmother

Theresa Vallone
Port Charlotte Lodge #2507

Chicken Potacchio
(Chicken with Red Wine Vinegar, Marchigana Style)

1 frying chicken cut into as many
   small pieces as possible
2 tbsp. Rosemary leaves
6-8 tbsp. olive oil

20 garlic cloves, peeled
   to the last thin skin
1/2 cup red wine vinegar
salt/pepper

In a heavy cast aluminum fry pan with a tight cover, heat olive oil. Add chicken, salt and pepper. Cook chicken quickly to a nice golden brown, stirring often. Add garlic, rosemary and vinegar. Lower heat, cover and let cook gently for 15-20 minutes. When chicken is fork tender, remove cover, turn up heat to reduce liquid in pan. Stir chicken pieces until well coated in pan juices. Serve with crescia and sauteed escarole.

Origin: Family favorite.

Rose Marie Boniello
Sgt. F. M. Bonanno Lodge #2549

Chicken Pizzaiola

2 lbs. chicken breast and thighs
4 large baking potatoes, quartered
1 large onion, sliced
1 can peas, drained
4 tbsp. parmesan cheese

1 can mushrooms, drained
1 large can plum tomatoes
4 tbsp. olive oil
1 tsp. oregano
salt/pepper

Arrange chicken, potatoes, peas, onion and mushrooms in a roasting pan. Pour tomatoes over top. Add salt, pepper, olive oil and cheese. Bake in a preheated oven at 375 degrees for 1 hour and 15 minutes. Serves 4.

Mildred Cagno
La Nuova Sicilia #1251

Chicken with Pickled Peppers

1 whole chicken
4 tbsp. olive oil
1/2 cup wine vinegar
1 jar sweet vinegar peppers, sliced
  (reserve vinegar in jar)
2 tbsp. parsley, chopped

4 garlic cloves, sliced
2 bay leaves
1 tsp. oregano
1/2 lb. mushrooms, sliced
salt/pepper

Cut chicken into serving pieces. Brown in oil and garlic. Add all other ingredients, cook uncovered for 45 minutes. Last 15 minutes add pickled peppers and reserved vinegar. Cover and steam for 15 minutes.

Marie Lotito
Rev. Albert B. Polombo Lodge #2512

Pollo al Vino Bianco
(Chicken with White Wine)

4 lb. roasting chicken
1/4 cup butter
2 tbsp. olive oil
1 garlic clove, chopped
2 celery stalks, finely chopped
Juice of 1/2 lemon
1 1/4 cups dry white wine
salt/pepper

1/4 cup flour seasoned with
  salt and pepper
1 medium onion, finely chopped
2 medium carrots, grated
1 slice ham, chopped
1/2 lb. mushrooms, sliced
1 cup chicken stock
1/2 tsp. Rosemary

Cut chicken into serving pieces, dust well with seasoned flour. Heat the butter and oil in a large pan. Add chicken and fry until brown and crisp all over. Remove to a plate. Add onion, garlic, carrots, celery and ham. Saute over low heat until soft (do not brown). Add lemon juice, mushrooms, wine, chicken stock, salt, pepper and rosemary. Bring to a high simmer. Add browned chicken, lower heat and cover the pan. Simmer very gently for 45 minutes or until the chicken is fork tender.

Maria Salerno
Veto Presutti Lodge #2463

Ricotta Stuffing
(12-15 lb. Turkey)

3 lb. ricotta cheese
1/2 cup grated cheese
6 oz. (1 stick) pepperoni
(cut in small pieces)

5 eggs
1 cup parsley, chopped fine

Put ricotta in a bowl, add eggs and stir until smooth. Add grated cheese, parsley and pepperoni and mix well. Stuff turkey before cooking.

Edythe M. Dell'Orfano
Sunrise/Tamarac Lodge #2542

Chicken alla Tetrazzini

5 lbs. roasting chicken
(cut into pieces)
1 tsp. salt
3/4 lb. spaghetti
1 lb. mushrooms, sliced thin
2 garlic cloves, minced

7 tbsp. butter
4 tbsp. flour
1 and 2/3 cup heavy cream
1/3 cup sherry
3/4 cup grated Parmesan cheese
salt to taste

Place chicken pieces in a kettle with boiling water to cover. Add salt and simmer covered 1 1/2 hours or until the chicken is tender. Allow the chicken to cool in the broth. Then remove skin and bones and cut meat into large pieces. Put the skin and bones back in the broth and let them cook until broth is reduced to 2 cups, strain.

Cook spaghetti al dente. Rinse in cool water, drain and set aside.

Saute mushrooms and minced garlic in 7 tablespoons of butter for 5 minutes. Blend in flour and add the hot strained reduced chicken broth a little at a time. Cook, stirring constantly, until the sauce is smooth and thick. Add the heavy cream and the sherry. Cook over a low heat until the cream and sherry are well blended into the sauce. Put a layer of spaghetti in the bottom of a buttered casserole then layer it with chicken and cover that layer with Parmesan and with some of the cream sauce. Repeat until casserole is full ending with the cream sauce and a final coating of Parmesan cheese over the top.

Bake in hot oven 450 degrees until the cheese is bubbling and browned. Serves 8-10.

Tana Lynn Boniello Mitchell
Sgt. F. M. Bonanno Lodge #2549

Contorni/
Salads and Vegetables

Old Fashioned Wild Dandelion Salad

1 large bunch dandelions
oil
salt/pepper

2 cloves garlic, chopped
wine vinegar

Wash dandelions thoroughly and drain. Cut into bite size pieces. Combine 3 parts oil to 1 part vinegar, garlic, salt and pepper. Shake well pour over dandelions and toss. Serve with crusty bread.

My father used to go picking dandelions. The children spent many hours cleaning them but were they ever delicious in a salad or cooked.

Mary Sorci
John Paul I Lodge #2427

Artichoke and Celery Salad

1 pkg. frozen artichoke hearts
2 tbsp. scallions, minced w/tops
1/2 tsp. dry mustard
6 tbsp. olive oil
1/4 tsp. pepper
lettuce/watercress

1 cup celery, chopped
2 whole pimentos, canned
 (cut in strips)
1/2 tsp. salt
2 tbsp. red wine vinegar

Combine artichokes, celery, onion and pimentos in a bowl. Mix mustard, salt, pepper, vinegar and oil in a small bowl. Pour over artichokes and toss gently. Cover bowl and refrigerate for 2 hours. Serve on individual salad plates lined with lettuce and watercress.

Mary Sorci
John Paul I Lodge #2427

Italian White Bean Salad

2 cans cannellini (white beans)
1/2 cup olive oil
1 tsp. basil

2/3 cup red onion, chopped
1 tsp. salt
2 tbsp. wine vinegar

Combine all ingredients and toss well. Refrigerate for several hours before serving.

Enez L. Bedard
Joseph A. Franzalia Lodge #2422

Mozzarella Salad

Dressing

1/2 cup olive oil	4 tbsp. white wine vinegar
1/2 tsp. salt	1/2 tsp. pepper
1/2 tbsp. oregano	3 tbsp. grated parmesan cheese
3 garlic cloves, crushed	

Salad

1 head lettuce, torn into pieces	1 cup green olives w/pimentos
2 cups black olives	(sliced)
(pitted and chopped)	2 cups mozzarella, shredded
10 plum tomatoes, sliced	

In large salad bowl, mix all ingredients. Pour dressing over salad. Serves 10

Lorraine Clementi
Unita Lodge #2015

Italian Chicken Salad

1 chicken, boiled as for soup	1 cup celery, coarsely chopped
1 cup onions, coarsely chopped	1/2 cup stuffed olives, sliced
2 tbsp. wine vinegar	4 tbsp. olive oil
1 tsp. oregano	1 tsp. sugar
1/2 cup black olives	salt/pepper
(pitted and crushed)	

Strain chicken. Reserve chicken stock for another meal. Debone and remove skin from chicken. Shred the meat. Saute onions, celery in olive oil a very short time. Add chicken, mix well with all other ingredients till heated.

May serve cold or hot.

Sarah M. Puleo
Unita Lodge #2015

Fresh Tomato Salad

4 large tomatoes
10-12 fresh basil leaves, cut up
1/4 cup Balsamic vinegar
1/4 tsp. oregano

1/2 red onion, diced fine
1/2 cup extra virgin olive oil
1 garlic clove, chopped
salt/pepper

Place the tomatoes, onion and garlic in a bowl, add seasonings then oil and vinegar.

Serve with Italian bread. Use the bread to soak up the juices from the salad.

Gladys W. Marino
Sunrise-Tamarac Lodge #2542

San Nazzaro Salad

4 large potatoes
8 stalks celery and leaves, sliced
1 medium onion, sliced
6 plum tomatoes, cut in quarters
4 garlic cloves, chopped
salt and coarse grind pepper

1 green pepper, coarsely chopped
1 red pepper, coarsely chopped
1 tsp. oregano
1/2 cup olive oil
1/4 cup wine vinegar

Boil potatoes in their jackets until cooked but firm about 25 minutes. Peel skins while still warm. Cut each potato into 8 pieces. In a large bowl toss potatoes with celery, onion, tomatoes, garlic, pepper, oregano, olive oil, wine vinegar, salt and pepper. Let set for 15-20 minutes. Add more oil if potatoes are dry.

Origin: My mother Rosina Boniello, San Nazzaro, Italy

John Boniello
Sgt. F. M. Bonanno Lodge #2549

Potato and String Bean Salad

1 lb. string beans	4 large potatoes
(cut in half)	(peeled and cubed)
1/4 cup olive oil	1 tbsp. wine vinegar
1/2 tsp. oregano	salt/pepper

Cook string beans in boiling water, until tender about 20 minutes. Boil potatoes until cooked but still firm, about 20 minutes.

Drain and combine vegetables in a serving bowl. Set aside to cool. Combine olive oil, vinegar and oregano. Pour over vegetables and season with salt and pepper. Toss gently and refrigerate until serving time. Makes 4 large servings.

Variation: **Add 2 hard boiled eggs, sliced**

Carmela Cannata
Unita Lodge #2015

Winter Potato Salad

4 large potatoes, boiled whole	8 celery stalks
4 garlic cloves, chopped	(sliced with leaves)
1 tsp. oregano	olive oil
dash wine vinegar	salt/pepper

Scrub potatoes, place in pot with water to cover. Boil about 25 minutes until cooked, but firm. Cool slightly, peel skin while still warm. Cut into medium size wedges. Toss potatoes with celery, garlic, oregano, salt and pepper with enough olive oil to moisten potatoes. Splash wine vinegar. Let set covered 15-20 minutes. Serve warm or room temperature. Serves 4-6

Origin: My Mother-in-law Rosina Boniello

Rose Marie Boniello
Sgt. F. M. Bonanno Lodge #2549

Olive Salad

1 lb. large green olives, pitted (slightly smashed)	2 medium carrots (sliced diagonally)
2 cups cauliflower florets	2-3 garlic cloves, chopped
1 tbsp. vinegar	2 tbsp. olive oil
3 tbsp. capers	4 pepperoncini
black pepper	(pickled peppers, mildly hot
1 tsp. oregano	1 cup celery (sliced diagonally)

Combine all ingredients. Mix very well. Store in air-tight container in refrigerator. Stir or shake from time to time. Keeps for weeks-the longer it marinates, the better it is.

Origin: Old Family Favorite

Angie Terrana
Unita Lodge #2015

Variation: Add

2-3 med. yellow or red onions (sliced)
1 red pepper (seeded and cut into strips)

Mary Sorci
John Paul I Lodge #2427

Olive Schiacciate
(Sicilian Olive Salad)

2 lbs. green Sicilian olives	2 large red peppers (cut in pieces)
2 garlic cloves, minced	1 carrot, sliced thin
1 head celery, diced	1/2 tsp. fennel seed
1 cup capers	1 tbsp. wine vinegar,
1 small onion, sliced	salt/pepper
1 cup olive oil	

Pound each olive until broken so that the pits show, but do not remove the pits. Place in large bowl and add all ingredients. Add salt only if needed. Mix well, cover and let stand in a cool place at least 24 hours before serving. Olives keep in a jar in the refrigerator for an indefinite time.

Origin: My Sicilian Neighbor

Rose A. Malzone
Ft. Lauderdale Lodge #2263

Holiday Olive and Tuna Salad

1 lb. Italian green olives
1 cup raisins
1 can tuna, with oil
1/2 cup onions, diced
1/2 cup pecans (optional)
vinegar

1 jar capers
1 cup almonds
1 cup celery, diced
1 bay leaf
1 tbsp. sugar
olive oil

Remove pits from olives and place in a bowl. Rinse capers and drain. Add the remaining ingredients and toss with vinegar and oil to taste. Refrigerate. Serve on a bed of lettuce.

Traditional to my family as a holiday salad.

Sara Friscia Capitano
La Nuova Sicilia Lodge #1251

Green Beans Marche Style

1 lb. green beans, fresh
3 garlic cloves, finely diced
3-4 tbsp. fresh mint leaves
  (finely chopped)

olive oil
wine vinegar
salt/pepper

To prepare beans, cut off tips and remove any strings. Break in half. Cook quickly in lightly salted water until crisp tender (do not overcook). Keep cover off to retain green color. Cool under running water to room temperature. Place in serving bowl. Drizzle olive oil, wine vinegar over top with diced garlic and chopped mint leaves.

Rose Marie Boniello
Sgt. F. M. Bonanno Lodge #2549

Zucchini Ripieni con Scampi
(Zucchini Stuffed with Shrimp)

4 medium zucchini
3 tbsp. lemon juice
1 cup shrimp, cooked / chopped
3 tbsp. Italian dressing
salt/pepper

1/4 cup grated cheese
2 medium tomatoes, cut wedges
1 can olives, pitted
1/8 tsp. garlic powder

Scrub zucchini very well with vegetable brush. Place in a large saucepan, add just enough cold water to cover. Bring to boil, reduce heat and simmer for 10 minutes or until tender.

Drain zucchini, let cool and then cut in half lengthwise; scoop out and reserve center. Brush cut side of zucchini with lemon juice. Chop zucchini centers coarsely. In small bowl, combine chopped zucchini, shrimp, Italian dressing, garlic powder, salt and pepper. Fill zucchini with shrimp mixture. Sprinkle some of the grated cheese, refrigerate at least 1 hour before serving.

Arrange tomato wedges and olives around zucchini for garnish. Pass more Italian dressing. Serves 8.

Laura D. Spoto
La Nuova Sicilia Lodge #1251

Calamari Salad

2 lbs. cleaned squid, cut in rings
1 lemon, squeezed
2 garlic cloves, diced fine
1 small red onion, chopped fine
1/2 tsp. oregano
1 lemon, sliced

1/2 cup olive oil
1/4 cup white wine vinegar
1/2 cup celery, chopped fine
1/2 tsp. basil
salt/pepper
2 tbsp. parsley, minced

Wash, clean, cut squid into rings. In a sauce pan bring lightly salted water to a boil and add squid rings and tentacles. Boil for 2-3 minutes, or until squid firms up. Chop up tentacles and triangular fins. Put into bowl with oil, lemon juice, garlic, celery, onion and spices. Mix well and refrigerate for 24 hours before serving.

Before serving sprinkle with parsley; garnish with lemon slices. Serves 6.

Victoria R. Casario
Jerry Barletta Lodge #2502

Broccoli Salad

1 bunch broccoli	olive oil
salt	juice of 1 lemon
fresh ground pepper, optional	1 red roasted pepper or
3 garlic cloves, chopped	(1 jar of pimento)

Peel stems, split broccoli with stems into large spears. One spear per serving. Steam in salted water until cooked but firm. Refresh with cool water, drain. Arrange broccoli on a serving platter, sprinkle with garlic and decorate with pepper slices.

Drizzle olive oil, lemon juice and ground pepper over top. Garnish with lemon peel. Marinate for one hour and serve at room temperature.

Jean Boniello
Sgt. F. M. Bonanno Lodge #2549

Eggplant Salad

1 or 2 eggplants	2 green peppers
2 eggs, beaten	1 large onion, sliced
1 cup bread crumbs	grated parmesan cheese
oregano	wine vinegar
salt/pepper	oil for frying

Slice unpeeled eggplant crosswise. Dip in egg then bread crumbs. Fry in hot oil. Drain on paper toweling. Layer eggplant in a salad bowl, then layer green peppers sliced in circles, next large onion sliced in circles and sprinkle grated cheese, black pepper and oregano. Sprinkle wine vinegar. Repeat each layer. Topping with onion, pepper and lots of cheese. Make the day before so that flavors will blend and the vinegar will seep through.

May also be used as an appetizer.

Flo Carbone
Sunrise-Tamarac Lodge #2542

Eggplant Parmigiana

2 large eggplants
6-8 eggs, beaten (with
   (1/2 cup grated cheese)
Marinara Sauce
salt/pepper

2 cups bread crumbs
16 oz. mozzarella, sliced thin
Olive oil for frying
8 oz. sliced mushrooms
   (optional)

Peel the skin from eggplants. Slice eggplant in half, then into slices, 1/4" thick. Dip eggplant in egg mixture and then roll in bread crumbs. Fry until light brown.

In baking pan put a layer of eggplant, sauce and mozzarella cheese, make layers until pan is full. Top with mozzarella, grated cheese and sauce. Mushroom can be added for taste.

Bake in 350-degree oven for 35 minutes until cheese melts.

Virginia A. Papale
Sunrise-Tamarac Lodge #2542
Josephine Furnari
Charles Bonaparte Lodge #2504

Whole Stuffed Eggplant in Tomato Sauce

1 large eggplant
10 pieces of Parmesan cheese
   (1" cubes)
16 oz. can crushed tomatoes
Olive oil
6 cups cooked rice

6 garlic cloves, cut in half
2-3 stalks of celery
   (cut in 1/2" pieces)
1/2 tsp. sweet basil
salt/pepper

Cut ends off of eggplant, peel and then stand eggplant up and cut slits about 1/4" all around but not through bottom. Stuff slits with garlic, cheese and celery. Brown eggplant in skillet on all sides with a little oil. Place eggplant in pot with tomatoes, add salt, pepper and sweet basil. Cook slowly on top of stove until tender about 1/2 hour. Slice eggplant, pour sauce over rice and serve.

Origin: Sicily, my mother's recipe

Rose J. LaPorta
Port Charlotte Lodge #2507

Stuffed Rolled Eggplant

2 large eggplants

Egg Mixture

3 eggs
1 cup milk
2 tsp. garlic, chopped
2 tsp. onion, chopped

1 tsp. parsley, chopped
flour for dredging
oil for frying

Cheese Filling

1 1/2 lb. Ricotta
2 eggs
1 1/2 tsp. garlic powder
1/2 tsp. onion powder
2 tsp. parsley, chopped

8 oz. mozzarella, shredded
salt\pepper
1/8 tsp. nutmeg (optional)
1/4 cup Parmesan cheese
Marinara sauce

Peel and slice eggplant lengthwise into 16 slices, about 1/8" thick. Soak in salt water for 30 minutes. Drain well, pat dry. Dip eggplant into flour then egg mixture. Fry in medium hot oil until golden brown, drain over several layers of absorbent paper.

Mix cheese filling, set aside. In a casserole dish, spread Marinara sauce thinly on bottom. Place a spoonful of cheese mixture on each slice of eggplant, roll up in jelly roll fashion and place seam side down in prepared casserole dish. Spoon more sauce on top of each roll and sprinkle with Parmesan cheese. Bake in hot oven, uncovered, for 14-18 minutes. Serves 8.

Dr. James Spina
Justin Antonin Scalia Lodge #2235

Eggplant alla Vesuviana

10 baby eggplants
1/2 cup black olives, diced
6-8 basil leaves

5 ripe tomatoes, peel/chop
1/4 cup capers
4 garlic cloves, chopped

Cut 8 of the 10 eggplants in half (lengthwise). Remove pulp carefully, leaving a shell. Fry eggplant shells in small amount of oil (preheated) until golden brown, put fried shells aside, retain oil in pan. Dice the remaining 2 eggplants and reserved pulp. Saute in oil until golden brown. Remove the eggplant and reserve. In the same pan cook the tomatoes to form a sauce. Add the reserved eggplant to the sauce with the capers, basil, garlic and olives - cook ingredients with the sauce for 2-3 minutes. Stuff the shells with cooked ingredients lay the shells in a baking pan. Bake at 350 degrees for 5-7 minutes. Serves 8.

Suzi Vargas
Sgt. F. M. Bonanno Lodge #2549

Parmigiana di Melanzane Bianca
(Baked Eggplant Parmesan)

1 eggplant, peeled	1/2 lb. mozzarella, shredded
6 eggs, beaten	6 tbsp. olive oil
1/2 cup Parmesan cheese	pepper
6-8 large basil leaves, chopped	

Slice eggplant 1/4" thick. Fry in hot oil quickly to soften. Do not overcook. Add oil as needed. In a baking dish, alternate layers of eggplant, mozzarella, fresh basil and Parmesan cheese. Add pepper to beaten eggs and pour over layered eggplant. Bake moderate oven 350 degrees until eggs are set and eggplant is tender, about 20-25 minutes. Serve hot or cold

Origin: My cousin, Cinza De Rosa, Salerno, Italy

Rose Marie Boniello
Sgt. F. M. Bonanno Lodge #2549

Eggplant Parmigiana Siciliana Style ✗

1 large eggplant	Marinara sauce
Oil for frying	1 cup Parmesan cheese
salt/pepper	

Peel eggplant, cut lengthwise in thin slices. Layer eggplant in a colander, sprinkle each layer lightly with salt. Let stand about 20 minutes to remove extra moisture. Rinse eggplant gently, pat dry on paper towel. Fry eggplant in hot oil until golden brown. Drain on paper towels.

In a baking dish, spread a thin layer of sauce, layer of eggplant and a sprinkle of cheese. Repeat layers ending with sauce.

At this point, eggplant may be covered and refrigerated to be used at room temperature for sandwiches, layered on hot pasta or as an appetizer. It will keep up to 10-12 days. It can also be baked at 350 degrees about 15-20 minutes and served hot.

Dora Battaglia
Lake Worth/Boynton Beach Lodge #2304
Philip Borgia
Sgt. F. M. Bonanno Lodge #2549

Variation
Add 1/2 cup fresh basil (chopped), in alternating layers.

Rose Van Saake
Sgt. F. M. Bonanno Lodge #2549

Baked Stuffed Eggplant and Tomato

2 medium eggplants   4 large firm tomatoes

Stuffing
4 cups bread crumbs   4 garlic cloves, minced
4 tbsp. parsley, chopped   1 cup Romano cheese, grated
4-5 tbsp. olive oil

Slice top from each tomato and reserve. Scoop pulp and seeds into a bowl. Cut up top and add to pulp. Slice eggplant in half lengthwise to form 1/2" shell, score eggplant lengthwise and crosswise with a knife being careful not to cut through. Scrape pulp out into bowl with tomatoes. Prepare oven pan so that eggplant and tomatoes will fit close together. Finely dice eggplant and tomato pulp and add to stuffing ingredients and mix well. Stuff eggplant and tomato shells and place in oiled oven pan. Drizzle olive oil over top. Bake uncovered 375 degrees about 45 minutes until fork tender and brown. Serve with crusty bread and salad for a Lenten meal or as a side dish for steak, pork chops or roasted chicken.

Origin: My mother, Elena Giuliani

Rose Marie Boniello
Sgt. F. M. Bonanno Lodge #2549

Eggplant Casserole with Basil

2 large eggplants, peeled   2 cups Marinara sauce
   and sliced   3/4 cup grated Parmesan cheese
1/2 cup olive oil   2 cups fresh basil, chopped
                                    (or 1 tbsp. dried basil)

Dip slices in oil on both sides and bake in single layers on large greased baking tray in preheated 400 degree oven, 20 minutes or until tender. Spread about 2 tbsp. tomato sauce in shallow 2 qt. baking dish, place 1/3 eggplant slices in single layers over sauce cover with layer of basil leaves or sprinkle with 1 tsp. of dried basil. Add half the Parmesan cheese, spread more sauce, follow with another layer of eggplant, basil, sauce and cheese. Bake in preheated oven 350 degrees for 15 minutes or until bubbling. Remove from oven - let stand 15 minutes before cutting and serving.

Rose Caggiano
Port Charlotte Lodge #2507

Cicoria con Fagioli
(Greens and Beans)

1 large bunch dandelion, endive
    escarole or wild dandelion
2-4 tbsp. olive oil
salt/pepper

3 garlic cloves, chopped
1 can cannellini beans
    (undrained)

Clean and wash greens. Heat water to boiling. Drop in greens. Remove when tender, drain. Saute garlic in oil, add greens that have been drained and simmer. Add beans, season with salt and pepper and any other seasonings that you prefer.

My mom usually had some leftover spaghetti sauce in the refrigerator and she would add that to the beans and greens for a yummy dish.

When dandelions were in season, my dad would go to some field and pick them so we would have fresh greens and beans. Such a simple dish but I remember it so well and we all loved it.

Gloria (Scalzitti) Walker
Joseph A. Franzalia Lodge #2422

Giambotto
(Blend of Mixed Vegetables)

1 eggplant
    (unpeeled/cubed)
1 potato, peeled/cubed
2 or 3 stalks of celery
    (cut in 2" pieces)
1 garlic clove, chopped

1 or 2 medium zucchini
    (scrubbed/cubed)
1 green pepper, cubed
1 onion, chopped
2 or 3 cups Marinara Sauce

Heat Marinara sauce, add the potato and celery. Cook 15 minutes, then add the zucchini, pepper, onion and garlic. Cook until tender about 15-20 minutes longer. Serves 4.

Origin: My mother

Nancy Tarantino
Jerry Barletta Lodge #2502

Minestra
(Greens and Beans)

1 large bunch escarole (or curly endive)	1 can cannellini beans (undrained)
1/4 lb. pepperoni, sliced/quartered	1 tsp. salt
3 garlic cloves, halved	4 tbsp. olive oil

Wash greens with tap water mixed with a teaspoon of salt. Rinse and put greens into boiling water. Cook until tender (do not overcook). When draining greens leave a little water for juice and moisture.

In a small pan, add olive oil and sliced garlic. Fry for a few minutes until garlic is lightly browned. Put aside. Optional - leave garlic in olive oil or take it out.

In another small pan, cook cut pieces of pepperoni in 2-4 tbsp. water. (Flavor is lost from pepperoni if too much water is used). Let boil for 2 minutes take out pepperoni, add garlic and olive oil mixture.

In a larger pan, mix together greens, olive oil and pepperoni. Let it come to a slow boil then add beans and slightly stir. Enjoy with or on top of Italian bread.

Joe & Antoinette Ciarciaglino
O.S.I.A. Lodge #321
Schenectady, New York
Submitted by Unita Lodge #2015

Minestra Palermitana
(Stewed Vegetables)

1 lb. peas, fresh-shelled	1 lb. Fava beans, fresh-shelled
1 lb. asparagus (fresh, cut in pieces)	6 small artichokes, hearts (leaves near hearts)
1 small onion, cut in pieces	1 tbsp. tomato paste
1/2 lb. small shells (cook half the time)	parsley salt/pepper

Brown onions in oil until wilted in a medium pot. Add all vegetables, tomato paste, salt, pepper and parsley flakes. Cover with water and let cook until tender (about 1/2 hour). Add pasta to the vegetables, stirring until it is a little dry.

Origin: Palermo, Italy

Dora Battaglia
Lake Worth/Boynton Beach Lodge #2304

Minestra d' Abruzzi
(Soup or Stew Type Dish)

1 ham bone
1/4 cup oil
2 carrots, chopped
1/4 cup parsley, minced
1/2 cup lentils
1 fennel bulb, chopped
1/2 lb. fresh spinach, shredded
1 cup fresh or frozen lima beans

1/4 cup lean salt pork, chopped
2 cloves of garlic, minced
16 oz. can cannellini beans
4 medium tomatoes, chopped
2 cups fresh or frozen peas
1/2 lb. wide noodles
    (broken into small pieces)

Simmer ham bone for 2 hours in water to cover. Remove bone from stock, trim meat from bone in pieces and return to stock. Set aside until needed.

Heat oil in soup pot, cook salt pork until crisp and then add carrots, garlic and parsley and saute a few minutes. Add remaining ingredients except spinach and noodles. Pour in reserved ham stock cover and simmer 1 hour. Add spinach and cooked noodles, simmer another 10 minutes. Serve with grated Parmesan cheese.

Mary A. Sorci
John Paul I Lodge #2427

Green Beans Italiano

3 lbs. string beans
3/4 cup grated Locatelli cheese
1/2 cup olive oil

1/2 cup parsley, chopped
1 cup plain bread crumbs
9 garlic cloves

Steam beans cook firm (do not overcook) and drain. Heat olive oil, saute garlic and parsley until tan. Add beans and stir two minutes. Remove from heat, add cheese and bread crumbs, toss to coat beans.

Origin: My mother - Villa SanJuan, Italy

Jack Calabro
Key West Lodge #2436

Italian Beans with Pesto

2 lbs. fresh green beans
1/4 tsp. salt
1 cup basil leaves, packed
2 tbsp. pine nuts

1/4 cup olive oil
1 large garlic clove, mashed
1/4 cup parsley leaves
1/4 cup Parmesan cheese

Parboil the beans and drain. Make the pesto by putting oil, salt, garlic, basil, parsley and nuts in a blender and puree. Add cheese and blend again. Dilute as needed with more oil and a little hot water. Toss sauce with beans and serve at room temperature. Serves 4-6.

Renata Curcio Rathmann
La Nuova Sicilia Lodge #1251

Scarciofoli Mondolfo Style
(Stuffed Artichoke)

Large long stemmed artichoke
1/2 cup water

2 tbsp. olive oil
salt/pepper

Bread Crumb Stuffing
1/2 cup bread crumbs
1 tbsp. broad leaf parsley
   (chopped)

1 garlic clove, chopped
2 tbsp. Parmesan cheese
salt/pepper

Remove hard outer leaves, cut off tips and cut stem to form an even base. Peel stems, dice and add to stuffing. Tap artichokes on a board, upside down so leaves spread a little, wash in running water, place upside down to drain. Spread leaves open and stuff with bread crumb mixture, working in layers. Place artichokes in a heavy pan with a tight fitting lid so artichokes are crowded together. Drizzle some olive oil (about 1 tbsp. each artichoke).

Mix olive oil, water, salt and pepper and pour into bottom of pan to steam artichokes. Place on top of stove on medium heat, with tight lid. Check artichokes every 10 minutes, pour more water as needed. Use a bulb baster to bring juice over top of the artichokes to moisten bread crumbs. Continue to add water until artichokes are tender. Test by pulling leaves, if leaves pull easily they are done. It takes about an hour or less depending on size and toughness of leaves. Serve one to a person as an accompaniment to steak, pork chops or roasted chicken. Can also be served as an appetizer. Delicious hot, room temperature or cold.

Origin: Grandmother Elena Giuliani

Rosalene Boniello Feller
Submitted by John Boniello
Sgt. F. M. Bonanno Lodge #2549

Frittedda
(Stewed Artichokes Sicilian Style)

1 bunch scallions, chopped
4 fresh small artichokes, chopped
   (or artichoke hearts)
1 lb. fresh fava beans, shelled*
l lb. fresh peas, shelled*
2 tsp. fresh lemon juice

1/4 cup olive oil
1 cup water
1 lb. pasta (Ditali) cooked
grated Romano cheese
salt/pepper
grated nutmeg (optional)

Use small artichokes. Trim and cut each one into eighths. Drop into water with lemon juice until all prepared.

Lightly saute onion in olive oil, add artichokes, cook a few minutes longer, add water. Bring to a boil and add peas, fava beans. salt, pepper and nutmeg cover and simmer for 20 minutes until vegetables are tender. Add more water during cooking, if necessary. Serve over hot pasta. Pass the Romano cheese. Serves 4.

* May use frozen fava beans and peas.

Variation
Frittedda may be served hot or cold as a vegetable dish or appetizer. To serve cold, stir in the following ingredients before cooling the dish.

4 mint leaves, chopped
1 tsp. wine vinegar
4 tsps. sugar

Mildred Cagno
La Nuova Sicilia Lodge #1251

Stuffed Artichokes
(Modern Version)

2 boxes frozen artichoke hearts
1 tsp. garlic powder
1/2 tsp. basil
Juice from one large lemon

6 slices bread (cubed)
1/3 cup olive oil
1/2 cup Parmesan cheese

Thaw and place artichoke hearts in 9" x 13" baking pan with bread cubes on top. Mix together other ingredients and pour over artichokes, salt and pepper to taste. Cover with foil and bake at 350 degrees for 30 minutes - uncover and bake another 10 minutes.

Origin: My mother-in-law, Grace DeLorenzo Croce

Shirley C. DeLorenzo
Joseph A. Franzalia Lodge #2422

Stuffed Zucchini

4 medium zucchini
1/4 cup onion, diced
1/2 cup Italian bread crumbs
1/2 cup mozzarella, shredded

1/2 lb. hot Italian sausage
1 garlic clove, crushed
1/4 cup Parmesan cheese

Cook zucchini in boiling water for 5 minutes, drain. Let cool, cut zucchini in half lengthwise, scoop out pulp leaving 1/4" shell. Place shells in a lightly oiled 13" x 9" x 2" baking pan. Mash pulp, drain well and set aside.

Remove casings from sausage. Cook sausage, onion, and garlic in a skillet until sausage is browned stirring to crumble sausage. Drain fat. Combine sausage mixture, pulp, bread crumbs and cheese. Mix well. Spoon mixture into shells. Bake at 350 degrees for 10 minutes or until Zucchini is tender. Sprinkle with mozzarella cheese and bake an additional 5 minutes. Serves 4.

Virginia Minghella
Mike Accardi Lodge #2441

Stuffed Zucchini

6 medium zucchini
1 garlic clove, split
1 cup fresh tomatoes
   (peeled and chopped)
1 tsp. salt
1/2 cup grated Parmesan cheese

1/4 cup butter or margarine
1 medium onion, chopped
1 cup cooked rice
1/2 tsp. dried oregano
1/2 tsp. cayenne pepper

Wash zucchini, cut off stems and cut each in half crosswise. Cook zucchini in large saucepan with 1/2 tsp. of salt and a small amount of boiling water. Cook for 5 minutes or until just tender. Drain well, cool and scoop out seeds.

In a skillet saute garlic in hot butter until golden then discard, add onions and saute until golden. To onions, add tomatoes, rice, oregano, salt and cayenne toss with fork until well mixed. Preheat oven to 450 degrees. Sprinkle the insides of each zucchini lightly with salt. Fill zucchini with rice mixture and sprinkle with grated cheese. Arrange in a single layer in a buttered baking dish. Bake uncovered 15 minutes. Place under broiler several minutes to brown top. Serves 10 to 12.

Laura Spoto
La Nuova Sicilia Lodge #1251

Scarola Imbottita
(Stuffed Escarole)

1 large escarole	1/2 cup black pitted olives
2 garlic cloves, chopped	(chopped)
1 can anchovies, fillets	dash of pepper

Discard bruised outer leaves. Spread leaves to rinse (do not pull apart). Place all ingredients between leaves. The amount of each ingredient varies according to individual taste. Wrap string around escarole about 2 " from top secure ends together. Steam in 1/2 cup of water until tender (5-10 minutes).

Origin: Potenza

Edith Cuccinelli
Sgt. F. M. Bonanno Lodge #2549

Stuffed Escarole

2 heads escarole	2 carrots, cut in sticks
(wash thoroughly and remove	
white center - use for salad)	

Stuffing mixture

1 garlic clove, crushed	1 can anchovies (2 oz.) fillets
1 tbsp. capers and/or pignoli	1 1/2 tbsp. grated cheese
1 egg	12 pitted Italian green olives
1/2 loaf Italian bread	(cut in half)
(softened in water)	fresh parsley, chopped

Open escarole and place stuffing mixture in center, gather top leaves and tie with string. Place escarole in dutch oven cover with chicken broth and simmer with carrot sticks until just tender. Remove string. Can be served with any fish entree, escarole salad or antipasto and, of course, with the carrot sticks. Make garlic bread with the other 1/2 of the Italian bread.

This is a recipe handed down from my Grandmother.

Yolanda V. Tina
Giordano Sons of Italy Lodge #2572

Stuffed Escarole Leaves

2 heads escarole
6 tbsp. olive oil
4 anchovy fillets, chopped
1/2 tbsp. parsley, minced
4 black olives, pitted/chopped
1 tbsp. pine nuts, optional
salt/pepper

1/2 lb. ground beef or Italian
    sausage (remove casing)
1 garlic clove, chopped
1/2 cup bread crumbs
4 green olives, pitted/chopped
3 tbsp. water

Discard wilted outer leaves. Wash heads under cold running water (I put a little flour in the water and all the sand goes to the bottom of the pot). Brown meat in oil over low flame for 10 minutes stirring occasionally. If sausage is being used, reduce oil to 2 tbsp. Remove meat from stove, add anchovies, garlic, parsley, crumbs, olives, pine nuts, dash of salt and pepper and mix thoroughly.

Drain escarole (I separate several leaves and wilt them in simmering water so that leaves are still firm, then drain). Hold leaves in your hand and put a small amount of filling on the leaves then roll the leaves with the filling into small rolls. Place stuffed rolls in a pan close together. Sprinkle with balance of oil and water, cover tightly and cook over medium flame until tender (18-20 minutes). Watch carefully, and add a little more liquid if necessary. Remove carefully from pan with pancake turner and serve immediately. Serves 6.

Rita J. Ricci
John Paul I Lodge #2427

Potatoes alla Angelina

8 large potatoes
    (peeled & quartered)
4 large bell peppers, quartered
salt/pepper

1-2 sticks margarine
    (cut in 1" pieces"
4 large onions, sliced
Dash of paprika

Place potatoes, onions and bell peppers in open baking pan. Sprinkle paprika, add margarine, salt and pepper. Cover with foil and bake at 350 degrees for 30 minutes. Stir, remove foil and cook 15 minutes uncovered.

My original recipe. It is over 40 years old. Everyone liked it so much, that it was called Potatoes alla Angelina, after me.

Angelina (Angie) C. Demmi
Unita Lodge #2015

Casseruola di Patate ☆
(Potato Casserole)

8 large potatoes, peeled
3 eggs, beaten
5 tbsp. butter or margarine
1/2 cup milk

1/2 lb. mozzarella, cubed
1/2 cup Parmesan cheese
bread crumbs
salt/pepper

Boil potatoes until tender. Mash them and add butter, milk, eggs, grated cheese, salt and pepper. Beat until creamy and light. Add cubed mozzarella. Pour into a buttered 2 1/2 qt. casserole. Smooth top of mixture and sprinkle bread crumbs. Bake in 375 degree oven until top is golden brown and crusty about 25 minutes. Test with a toothpick if potatoes are dry. Serve hot.

Ann Lombardi
John Paul I Lodge #2427

Variation
Add to the above ingredients -

1 additional egg
1 cup ham, diced

1/2 cup pepperoni, diced
1 cup Swiss cheese, shredded

Marie Lotito
Rev. Albert B. Palombo Lodge #2512

Rapini e Pasta
(Broccoli Rabe with Pasta)

1 large bunch broccoli rabe
2 tbsp. olive oil
4-5 garlic cloves
1/2 cup grated cheese

2 (2 oz.) cans flat anchovies
1 lb. ziti or cavatelli
(cooked al dente)
red pepper (optional)

Separate broccoli rabe, rinse carefully several times to remove sand. Break off tough stems, discard. Cut stalks into thirds and drop into boiling water. Lower heat and cook gently 2-3 minutes. Do not overcook. Drain, reserving 1 cup water, set aside.

Anchovy sauce
Open anchovy cans, drain reserving 2 tbsp. oil. Cut fillets in thirds. Heat olive oil, saute garlic to a pale color, add cut anchovies and reserved oil. Saute additional 1-2 minutes. Add 1 cup reserved water from broccoli rabe. Pour vegetable and anchovy sauce over pasta. Toss and serve hot with grated cheese and hot pepper.

Elvira Pezzolla
Sgt. F. M. Bonanno Lodge #2549

Fried Celery

1 medium bunch celery
1 1/2 cups bread crumbs
2 tbsp. parsley, chopped
salt/pepper

2 eggs
6 tbsp. grated cheese
1 garlic clove, minced
olive oil

Separate celery stalks, scrub with a brush. Trim off root and any blemishes, remove strings. If too wide, cut in half and then into 3" pieces. Cook celery in boiling salted water, covered for 15 minutes or until tender. Drain.

In a shallow bowl, beat eggs, add garlic. In another bowl, combine bread crumbs, cheese, parsley, salt and pepper. Dip celery pieces in egg and dredge in bread crumb mixture. Heat oil in large skillet and saute celery pieces over low flame until golden brown on both sides. Add more olive oil if needed. Drain on absorbent paper. Serves 5-6.

Carmela Cannata
Unita Lodge #2015

Spinach Roll

3 lbs. potatoes
3 lbs. spinach
salt
1/2 cup Parmesan cheese

3 cups flour
3 eggs
butter
tomato meat sauce

Boil 3 lbs. potatoes (peel), drain and put through ricer, slowly knead flour into potatoes with 1 egg and salt. Spread the dough 1/2" thick on to a floured cheese cloth.

Prepare spinach by blanching in boiling water, drain, chop and saute in butter. Allow to cool then add 2 eggs, salt and Parmesan cheese. Spread spinach filling on to dough and using cheese cloth, roll into a log and tie both ends. Immerse log into salted boiling water and cook for 20 minutes. Let roll cool, then slice it, sprinkle with grated cheese and cover with a good meat sauce.

Origin: Trieste, Italy

Emilia Piuca
John Paul I Lodge #2427

Polpettine di Spinaci e Ricotta
(Spinach and Ricotta Balls)

2 cups cooked spinach
   (chopped/drained well)
1 egg
3 tsp. grated cheese
flour for coating

1/2 cup grated cheese
1/2 lb. ricotta
salt/pepper
Marinara sauce

Drain spinach well. Combine spinach, cheese, ricotta, egg and seasonings. Mix thoroughly. Shape into balls (1 heaping tablespoon mixture), roll each in flour then drop balls (5 at a time) into 3 qts. of boiling water and cook for 5 minutes (from the time balls rise to the surface). Lift balls out gently with a slotted spoon, place in a serving dish cover with tomato sauce and sprinkle with additional cheese. Serve immediately.

Rita J. Ricci
John Paul I Lodge #2427

Cannellini Beans ✷
(Baked Italian Beans with Sausage)

2 cans cannellini beans
1/4 lb. bacon
1 lb. sweet Italian sausage
   (sliced in 1" pieces)
basil

1 can tomato sauce
   (add 1 can water to sauce)
garlic powder
pepper
parsley

Drain beans in strainer, do not wash. Set aside. Fry bacon until well cooked. Put beans, tomato sauce, water and all pan drippings into casserole dish leaving room for sausage. Saute sausage until cooked, add to casserole with seasonings, mix. Bake in a 350 degree oven for 30 minutes.

Enjoy with a salad and crusty bread. Serves 4 for main dish, and 6-8 for side dish.

Origin: Family recipe, De Jon/Salerno

Gladys Marino
Sunrise-Tamarac Lodge #2542

Broccoli Sicilian Style

1 small bunch broccoli
4 tbsp. olive oil
1 large onion, sliced
10 pitted black olives
   (cut into pieces)
4 anchovy fillets, cut in pieces

1/2 tsp. salt
1/2 tsp. pepper
1/4 lb. Provolone cheese
   (finely diced)
1 cup dry red wine

Clean broccoli and cut into very thin slices. Pour 1 tablespoon olive oil in bottom of pan, place thin slices of onion, some olives, some anchovy and one layer of broccoli. Add a sprinkle of cheese, salt and pepper and sprinkle with olive oil. Repeat procedure until all ingredients are used. Pour remaining olive oil over top, add wine. Cover pan and cook over low heat about 30 minutes or until broccoli is tender. Serves 4.

Frank W. Ricci
Justin Antonin Scalia Lodge #2235

Cavolfiore al Forno
(Baked Italian Cauliflower)

1 large head cauliflower
1/2 cup bread crumbs
1/4 cup olive oil

2 tbsp. olive oil
1/2 cup grated cheese

Wash and clean cauliflower, break into flowers. Boil for 6 minutes in salt water until half done. Drain. Coat bottom of pan, with 2 tbsp. olive oil, arrange cauliflower on bottom of pan. Combine crumbs and cheese sprinkle over flowers. Season with pepper and garlic powder. Drizzle 1/4 cup of olive oil on top. Bake 350 degrees for 30 minutes. If it becomes dry, add 1/4 cup of water. Serves 6.

Pauline P. Parker
Joseph A. Franzalia Lodge #2422
Margaret Scarfia
John Paul I Lodge #2427

Cauliflower alla Romagna

1 head cauliflower
1/2 tsp. salt
2 eggs, slightly beaten
1 tbsp. Parmesan cheese

2/3 cup bread crumbs
1/4 tsp. pepper
1/4 cup milk
Oil for frying

Cut cauliflower into 2" floweretes, then parboil cauliflower in a large amount of water (do not overcook).

Mix bread crumbs, grated cheese, salt and pepper set aside. Combine eggs and milk coat flowerets with egg mixture and then roll in crumb mixture. Fry in single layer 2-4 minutes until golden brown turning occasionally. Drain remove to absorbent paper. Continue to fry until all flowerets are browned. About 4 servings.

Theresa Viscusi
Township Sons of Italy Lodge #2624

Stuffed Italian Peppers

12 Italian frying peppers
1/2 cup grated cheese
1 tbsp. pepper
olive Oil

2 cups bread crumbs
1 tsp. salt
2 garlic cloves, chopped

Remove stem and seeds from peppers and set aside. Combine bread crumbs, cheese, salt, pepper and garlic. Add oil (enough to make stuffing). Stuff peppers with bread crumb mixture. Coat bottom of baking pan with a little oil and bake at 400 degrees for approximately 1/2 hour.

Phyllis Leotta
Port Charlotte Lodge #2507

Roasted Fried Peppers

3 large peppers
2 tbsp. olive oil
1/2 tsp. salt
1/2 tsp. pepper

1/2 cup flour
1 egg, slightly beaten
1 cup olive oil
4 oz. seasoned bread crumbs

Roast peppers in very hot oven (450 degrees) for 10 minutes or until peppers peel easily. Peel and remove seeds and cut into thin slices. Place in dish, add oil, salt and pepper and let stand 1/2 hour. Drain off oil, roll in flour, dip into egg and fry in very hot olive oil until golden brown. Sprinkle bread crumbs on top of peppers, place under broiler for 1 minute.

Vincent Lupo
Justin Antonin Scalia Lodge #2235

Crema di Cipolle
(Creamed Onions)

6 cups onions, sliced
3 tbsp. flour
1 cup chicken broth
grated Parmesan cheese
1 1/2 cups croutons

1/4 cup butter or margarine
2 cups milk or cream
snipped parsley
dash of ground nutmeg
salt/pepper

Saute onion in butter or margarine until deep gold, sprinkle with nutmeg, salt and pepper blend in flour. Slowly add milk and cook, stirring occasionally until slightly thickened, stir in chicken broth cook 5 minutes longer. Adjust seasoning and serve with a topping of parsley, cheese and croutons. Serves 6.

Origin: Piemonte, Torino

Alfa Rosso
Sgt. F. M. Bonanno Lodge #2549

Pasticcetto di Bietole
(Swiss Chard Patties)

2 cups cooked swiss chard
  (chopped)
1/4 cup Parmesan cheese
olive oil

1 cup bread crumbs
1 egg, slightly beater
salt/pepper

Drain swiss chard well. Mix thoroughly crumbs, cheese, egg, salt, pepper and swiss chard. Shape into 3" patties about 1/2" thick and fry in hot oil until golden brown on both sides. Serves 4.

Rita J. Ricci
John Paul I Lodge #2427

Piselli alla Fiorella
(Peas, Prosciutto and Onions)

2 lbs. fresh peas, or
  1 pkg. frozen peas, thawed
1 medium onion, chopped
3 tbsp. butter

6 thin slices of prosciutto
  (chopped)
dash of pepper

Saute onion in butter until soft and wilted, do not brown. Add prosciutto (saute), stirring for about 3 minutes. Add peas and pepper. Stir and cook until peas are tender, about 5 minutes.

Origin: My cousin, Fiorella Giuliani - Battepaglia, Italy

Rose Marie Boniello
Sgt. F. M. Bonanno Lodge #2549

DOLCI/
DESSERTS

Cucciddata
(Sicilian Fruit Filled Pastry)

Dough

8 cups flour	1 cup shortening or lard
3 cups confectioners sugar	1/2 tsp. salt
2 tbsp. baking powder	2 egg yolks, beaten
2 tsp. vanilla	cold water, as needed

Combine flour, confectioners sugar, baking powder and salt. Cut in shortening, add yolks and vanilla. Blend and knead. If a little dry, add cold water a tablespoon at a time to form a pliable dough. Cut into four parts, knead each well, cover and let rest 1 hour.

Filling

2 lbs. dry figs	3/4 cup candied citron, chopped
1/4 cup Brandy or	1/2 cup toasted almonds, chopped
sweet Vermouth	1/4 cup dark molasses
1 cup applesauce	1/2 cup walnuts, chopped
1 1/2 tbsp. orange rind	1/4 cup dates, chopped
(finely chopped)	1 tsp. nutmeg
3/4 cup raisins, chopped	1 tsp. cinnamon
6 oz. chocolate bits	1 tbsp. vanilla or almond extract
1 tsp. allspice	

Immerse dry figs in hot water for about 5 minutes, drain, remove stem and chop. Mix with all other filling ingredients and refrigerate 1-2 hours.

Roll out dough to a rectangular sheet to 1/8-1/4" thickness. Cut into strips 4" wide. Place filling along edge of strip to about 1 1/2-2" to the edge. Roll dough over to form a tube. Press edges together. Cut diagonally into 2-3" pieces, cut a slit on top. Place on ungreased cookie sheet. **Do not crowd.** Bake in preheated oven 350 degrees for 15-20 minutes, until golden in color.

Icing

1/2 box confectioners sugar, 1 egg white, juice of 1/2 lemon and 1 tsp. vanilla. Blend all together to form a soft icing. Spread on warm cookies. Return to oven for a few minutes to dry icing.

Origin: Traditional to my family

Rose Van Saake
Sgt. F. M. Bonanno Lodge #2549

Cucciddata
(Italian Filled Cookies)

Dough

5 1/2 cups flour
1/2 cup sugar
6 tsp. baking powder
1/4 tsp. salt

2 tbsp. anisette liqueur
6 large eggs
2 tsp. vanilla
1 lb. butter or margarine

Mix flour, sugar, salt and baking powder in large bowl. Cut in butter until coarse meal. Make well add eggs and vanilla until mixture leaves side of bowl. Knead until smooth, set aside.

Filling

3 cups raisins
1 lb. pkg. figs
1/2 cup brown sugar

1 cup walnuts
1 tsp. cinnamon
2 tbsp. water

Chop or grind fruit and nuts. Add cinnamon, brown sugar and water. Cook over low heat until fruit is soft and filling has thickened. Set aside, cool. Roll dough thin, cut in 2" circles with cookie cutter. Put 1 tablespoon of filling in center, fold and seal edges. Bake in 375 degree oven until golden brown.

Lee Fulco
John Paul I Lodge #2427

Bitinibitie
(Raisin Pastries)

Dough

2 cups flour
1 tsp. salt
1 egg, beaten

2/3 cup shortening
5-8 tbsp. cold water

Mix flour and salt, cut in shortening, add egg and water to form pastry dough. Shape into a ball and let rest, covered.

Raisin Filling

3 cups raisins
1 cup nuts
1/4 cup citron (optional)
1/4 cup honey

1 tsp. vanilla
1 tsp. cinnamon
2-3 tbsp. grape jelly
1 egg, beaten

Chop or grind raisins, nuts and citron. Add honey, vanilla and cinnamon. Mix well, then add enough jelly to moisten. Roll dough thin, cut into 4" circles. Place 1 tbsp. filling on each circle. Fold to form half circle, seal edges. Make 3 slits on top, brush with beaten egg. Bake 450 degrees, 18-20 minutes.

Origin: My parents brought the recipe from Calabria, Italy.

Lucy Barbieri
John Paul I Lodge #2427

Easy Italian Cookies ☆

1/2 lb. butter, softened
2 large eggs, beaten
1 cup sugar

4 cups flour
2 tbsp. baking powder
2 tbsp. vanilla

Cream butter and sugar, add eggs and flavoring. Mix well. Blend in flour and baking powder. Work to form a soft pliable dough.

Cut off pieces of dough, the size of a walnut, roll to about 1/2" thickness, then shape into a curved 'S' shape about 2 1/2" long or a straight 2 1/2" pencil shape. Bake in preheated oven 375 degrees until lightly brown about 15-20 minutes. Cookies may be iced or left plain.

Icing
1/2 box confectioners sugar
2 tbsp. milk

1 tbsp. anise extract

Blend sugar and anise extract, adding milk slowly to form a soft, smooth icing. Ice cookies while warm, sprinkle confettini over top.

Anna Guecia
John Paul I Lodge #2427

Comments: I shape my cookies into knots, bake, then frost with vanilla flavored sugar icing and sprinkle with confettini or colored sugar.

Mary Lozito
Rev. Albert B. Palombo Lodge #2512

Comments: My cookies are shaped into bows, braids or knots and I use anise flavoring in the icing.

Josephine Ragone
Jerry Barletta Lodge #2502

Comments: I break off pieces of dough, roll into a short pencil shape, then shape the dough around my finger to form a turban. I use fresh lemon juice to flavor the icing and top with red sprinkles.

Nancy Bonamo
Ft. Lauderdale Lodge #2263

Suziemella
(Suzie Cookies)

15 oz. Black Strap molasses
1 cup oil
2 eggs, beaten
1 cup sugar
1/2 tsp. baking soda
6-7 cups flour

1 tsp. salt
1 tbsp. black pepper
5 whole orange rinds, grated
(about 1/2 cup)
1 cup filberts, sliced

Mix molasses, oil, eggs, sugar, baking soda, salt, pepper and orange rind. Blend well. Add flour to form a dough that can be rolled. Oil fingers, take pieces of dough and roll like a pencil. Shape roll into a 4-5" S shape. Place a sliced filbert on top and bottom of S. Bake on a greased cookie sheet 375 degrees for about 15 minutes, until brown. *These are great wine 'dunkers'.*

Origin: Carmela Derrico

Ann Tosti Goodman
Lake Worth/Boynton Beach Lodge #2304

Walnut and Almond Cookies

3 cups flour
3 tsp. baking powder
1 tsp. salt
3 tbsp. shortening
4 eggs
3/4 cup sugar
1 1/2 cups toasted walnuts
(chopped)

1 tsp. allspice
1 tsp. nutmeg
2 tsp. almond extract
2 tsp. cinnamon
2 tsp. orange rind, grated
1 1/2 cups toasted almonds
(chopped)

Combine flour, baking powder and salt. Work shortening into flour. Beat eggs into sugar, then add to flour, beat until a smooth dough. Sitr in the spices, orange rind and nuts. Blend well. Let dough rest 30 minutes.

Moisten hands with oil, form 1 tablespoon of dough into a 1" ball. Place on a greased cookie sheet. Bake in a preheated oven 375 degrees for about 20 minutes.

Icing
Beat 2 egg whites and 1/4 cup fresh lemon juice together. Gradually add confectioners sugar to form a smooth consistency. Brush icing over hot cookies as they come from the oven.

Rose Van Saake
Sgt. F. M. Bonanno Lodge #2549

Biscotti con Pignoli

2 lbs. almond paste
1 1/2 cups confectioners sugar
8 egg whites (room temperature)
1 lb. pignoli (pine) nuts

1 1/2 cups sugar
2 tbsp. honey
1/4 tsp. vanilla

Cream together the almond paste, sugars and honey into a smooth batter. Beat the egg whites until stiff, then gradually mix into the batter, along with the vanilla. Spread the pignoli in a dish. Drop batter by teaspoonful into the nuts, then place onto a lightly greased cookie sheet at 1" intervals. Bake in preheated 350 degree oven for 12-15 minutes or until golden. Remove carefully from baking sheet with a spatula while still warm. Makes about 4 dozen.

Rose Malzone
Ft. Lauderdale Lodge #2263
Josoephine Bonfiglio
Sgt. F. M. Bonanno Lodge #2549
Rose Van Saake
Sgt. F. M. Bonanno Lodge #2549

Biscotti di Regina
(Regina Cookies)

2 cups flour
3/4 cup sugar
2/3 cup shortening
1 1/2 tsp. baking powder
1/2 cup sesame seeds

1/4 tsp. salt
2 egg yolks
1/4 cup milk
1 tsp. vanilla

Mix flour, baking powder and salt. Set aside. Cream sugar and shortening, blend until creamy. Add egg yolks, milk and vanilla. Stir in flour, blend and mix to a smooth dough.

Break off 1 rounded teaspoon of dough, roll in sesame seeds. Place 1/2" apart on cookie sheet. Bake 15-20 minutes in a preheated oven 375 degrees until brown. Makes 2 1/2 dozen.

Dottie Fisichella
John Paul I Lodge #2427

Comments: I roll pieces of dough into a rope 18" long and 1/2" thick, then cut into 1 1/2" pieces. Dip each piece in milk, then roll in sesame seeds. Great grandma, Abbate, made these cookies.

Marie Abbate
Lake Worth/Boynton Beach Lodge #2304

Italian Spice Cookies with Lemon Icing

1 cup raisins	3 tbsp. orange juice
3 1/4 cups flour	1 tsp. baking powder
1/2 tsp. baking soda	1 tsp. cinnamon
1 tsp. allspice	3/4 tsp. ginger
1/4 tsp. nutmeg	1 cup butter, softened
1 cup sugar	1 egg
2 tsp. vanilla	1 lemon rind, grated
1 orange rind, grated	

Glaze

1 1/2 cups confectioners sugar	3 tbsp. lemon juice
4 tbsp. candied fruit, optional	

Combine raisins and orange juice, set aside to plump.

Beat butter and sugar until creamy. Add the egg, vanilla and lemon and orange rind. Stir in 2 cups of flour, baking powder, baking soda, and spices. Then add raisins and juice. Add remaining flour, do not overbeat.

Shape dough into 1" in balls. Refrigerate dough briefly if it is too soft. Place balls 1" apart on lightly greased baking sheets. Bake in preheated 350 degree oven for 7-9 minutes, or until cookies feel nearly firm when gently pressed. Let cookies cool slightly on baking sheet then remove to wire racks. Prepare glaze by stirring together confectioners sugar and juice until mixture is smooth and thin. Drizzle glaze on the warm cookies, then lightly press on candied fruit or sprinkles. Makes 5 dozen cookies.

Rose Malzone
Ft. Lauderdale Lodge #2263

Italian Amaretti Cookies

3/4 cup almonds	2 egg whites
1/4 tsp. salt	1 cup sugar
1/2 tsp. almond extract	

Cover cookie sheet with a cut brown paper bag. Blanch almonds and grind fine. Beat egg whites and salt until frothy. Add sugar 1 teaspoon at a time, beat until stiff peaks form. Fold in almonds and extract. Drop by teaspoon onto brown paper. Keep them small and uniform in size. Bake at 350 degrees for 20 minutes until very light in color. Makes 3 dozen.

These are served at weddings, christenings and family get-togethers.

Mary Sorci
John Paul I Lodge #2427

Italian Frittelle

2 pkgs. active dry yeast	1 cup warm water
2-3 cups flour	1 tsp. salt
2 tsp. anise seeds	2 tbsp. Olive oil
1 cup dark, seedless raisins	1 cup oil for frying
1 1/2 cups honey	2 tbsp. lemon juice

Dissolve yeast in 1 cup of warm water. Combine flour, salt and anise seeds in a bowl. Gradually add the yeast and olive oil, mixing until a rather soft dough is formed. Turn out onto a floured board and knead for 10 minutes, until dough is smooth and elastic.

Scatter the raisins over the board and kead the dough over them until they have been incorporated. Shape dough into a ball, cover with a clean kitchen towel and let rise in a warm place for 1 hour, or until doubled in bulk.

With the palms of your hands, flatten the dough down to 1/2" thickness. Let rest, uncovered, for 15 minutes. Use a sharp knife to cut the dough into 36 diamonds. Heat oil and fry the diamonds, a few at a time, turning until golden brown on both sides. Transfer to a paper towel to drain.

Heat honey with 2 tablespoons of lemon juice and boil for just 3 minutes. Arrange fritelle on a serving place and pour the hot honey over them. Makes 36.

Origin: Mother's recipe

Rose Malzone
Ft. Lauderdale Lodge #2263

Sicilian Wedding Cookies ⭐

2 cups butter	4 tbsp. confectioners sugar
1 1/2 tsp. water	2 tsp. vanilla
2 cups flour	1 cup pecans, chopped

Cream butter and sugar. Add all other ingredients. Roll into small balls (a little larger than marbles) and place on non-greased cookie sheet. Chill for 1 hour. Bake 375 degrees for 15-20 minutes. Roll in powdered sugar while warm and again when cool. Yield 50 cookies.

Origin: "Mom" Pat Cavallaro

Marie Scarpelli
Sunrise-Tamarac Lodge #2542

Anisette Cookies ⭑

4 cups flour	6 tbsp. baking powder
1 cup sugar	3/4 cup oil
1/2 cup milk	1 tbsp. anise extract
2 eggs, large	

In a large bowl, mix flour, baking powder and sugar. Make a well in the center and add oil, milk, anise and eggs. Mix together until dough is sticky. Oil fingers and pinch off dough in 1" pieces. Roll in a ball and place on a lightly greased cookie sheet, 1" apart. Flatten top slightly. Bake at 375 degrees for 8 minutes. Dip cookies in icing while warm.

Icing
Blend in 1 tsp. anise extract and enough hot water to 1 cup confectioners sugar to form a smooth icing. Makes 40 cookies.

Connie Esposito
Sgt. F. M. Bonanno Lodge #2549

Pizzette di Cioccolata ⭑
(Italian Chocolate Cookies)

1 1/2 cups oil	8 cups flour
1 tsp. vanilla	1 cup sugar
2 cups milk	10 tsp. cocoa
3 eggs	8 tsp. baking powder
1 jar maraschino cherries	1 tsp. cinnamon
(chopped)	1 tsp. cloves
3 cups walnuts, chopped	

Mix flour, sugar, cocoa, baking powder, cinnamon and cloves, set aside.

Beat together oil, vanilla, milk, eggs and chopped cherries. When creamy mix with the dry ingredients, using hands to form cookie dough. Break off pieces of dough and roll into a ball about 1 1/2" round. Place 1" apart on a greased cookie sheet. Bake 10 minutes in a 375 degree oven. Bottom of cookie should be firm - **Do not overbake.** Makes 100 cookies.

Frosting

2 boxes confectioners sugar	3 tbsp. cocoa
1/2 cup butter, softened	milk as needed

Cream sugar, cocoa and butter, adding milk a tablespoon at a time until creamy consistency.

Origin: My mother made these cookies for showers and weddings.

Ellen C. Feigenbaum
Ft. Lauderdale Lodge #2263

Ricotta Cookies ☆

1/2 cup butter, softened
1/4 cup ricotta
1 tsp. vanilla
1 cup sugar

1 egg, beaten
2 cups flour, sifted
1/2 tsp. baking soda
1/2 tsp. salt

Preheat oven to 350 degrees.

Blend butter with ricotta until creamy. Add vanilla, then add sugar gradually, beating until well blended. Add egg and slowly stir in dry ingredients, until well blended. Drop by teaspoon onto a lightly greased cookie sheet. Bake 10 minutes. Makes 30-36 cookies.

Rose Marie Tufarella
Sunrise-Tamarac Lodge #2542

Dark Almond Slices

1/2 cup vegetable oil
3 eggs, large
1 cup sugar
1 cup brown sugar
2 1/2 cups flour

2 tsp. baking powder
2 tsp. cinnamon
1/2 tsp. cloves
2 cups almonds, sliced
1 egg yolk, slightly beaten

Add oil to eggs, white and brown sugar, blend well. Combine flour, baking powder, cinnamon, cloves and almonds.

Mix all ingredients together. If dough is too soft, add more flour until dough does not stick to hands. Form into two loaves to fit a greased cookie sheet lengthwise. Brush top of loaves with egg yolk. Bake in preheated oven 375 degrees for 20-25 minutes. Slice loaves diagonally, 3/4" while still warm.

Grace De Bartolo
Sgt. F. M. Bonanno Lodge #2549
Millie Pietrini
Young Italians Lodge #2256

Variation
Omit cinnamon, cloves, sliced almonds. Add 1 tsp. allspice, 1 tsp. nutmeg and 2 cups whole almonds, toasted.

Jeanette D'Alessandro
Coral Springs Lodge #2332

Biscotti
(Toasted Cookie Slices)

3/4 cup butter	1/2 tsp. salt
1 cup sugar	1 tsp. anise seeds
4 eggs	1 cup almonds
3 cups flour	milk
3 tsp. baking powder	granulated sugar

Cream butter and sugar until light - add eggs, one at a time. Continue beating until very light and fluffy. Mix flour, baking powder, salt and anise seed together, then mix into creamed mixture. Stir in nuts, divide dough into fourths. Grease 2 cookie sheets. Form dough into 2 loaves, 1 1/2" wide and the length of each baking sheet. Bake at 350 degrees for 25-30 minutes. Remove from oven. Cut loaf diagonally into 3/4" slices. Place cut side down on cookie sheet, brush with milk and sprinkle with granulated sugar. Return to oven, bake 375 degrees, 10 minutes longer until toasted and crisp.

Jennie L. Albano
La Nuova Sicilia Lodge #1251

Variation
Omit anise seeds, milk and granulated sugar. Add 1 tsp. vanilla and toast almonds to a golden brown before adding to dough. Follow above directions for baking loaves. After loaves are cut diagonally, return to oven 10 minutes longer to a golden brown.

Mary A. Siligato
Submitted by Josephine Bonfiglio
Sgt. F. M. Bonanno Lodge #2549

Variation:
Omit anise seeds and chopped almonds. Add 1 1/2 tsp. vanilla and 1 tsp. of lemon and 1 tsp. orange rinds (grated). When baked, slice each roll diagonally and return to oven 5-10 minutes to brown.

Isabella Resta
John Paul I Lodge #2427

Chocolate Biscotti

2 cups hazelnuts, toasted
4 oz. unsweetened chocolate
3 eggs, separated
3 cups flour
1/2 tsp. baking powder

1/2 cup butter
1/2 tsp. vanilla
1 1/4 cups sugar, divided
1 egg white, lightly beaten

Finely chop 1/4 of the hazelnuts and coarsely chop the rest. Set aside. In a double boiler, melt butter and chocolate. Stir in vanilla and cool. Beat egg yolks with half the sugar until thick and pale. Fold in cooled chocolate mixture. In a separate bowl, beat 3 egg whites, gradually adding remaining sugar until stiff. Mix flour with baking powder and fold into liquid ingredients. Fold in all the nuts. With lightly floured hands, form dough into a loaf about 1 1/2" wide and 10" long. Place on a lightly greased baking sheet. Brush dough with egg white. Bake in preheated 350 degree oven for 45 minutes, or until dough is set. Remove loaf from baking sheet and cut on the diagonal into 1/2" thick slices.

Place slices on baking sheet, return to oven, and toast 5-8 minutes on each side, or until slightly dry. Makes about 30 cookies.

Rose Malzone
Ft. Lauderdale Lodge #2263

Biscotti all' Anici
(Anise Biscuits or Toast)

2 eggs
2/3 cup sugar

1 cup flour
1 tsp. anise seeds

Place eggs and sugar in bowl and beat well 10 minutes. Add flour slowly, blending gently and thoroughly. Add anise seeds. Butter and flour a loaf pan (9"x5"x3"), pour in batter and bake in preheated oven 375 degrees for 20 minutes.

Remove from pan (leave oven on), cut loaf into 1" slices and place slices on buttered baking sheet. Return to oven. Brown slices on both sides for about 5 minutes on each side. Makes about 20 biscuits.

Helen P. Mirabole
Unita Lodge #2015
Carmela Cannata
Unita Lodge #2015

Farfallette Dolci
(Fried Bow Wings or Bow Knots)

6 eggs
3 tbsp. granulated sugar
3 cups flour
1/2 tsp. orange flavoring
oil for frying

1 tsp. almond flavoring
1/2 cup confectioners sugar
1/4 tsp. salt
2 tbsp. butter, softened

Beat eggs, sugar, salt and flavorings. Place flour on board, cut in butter, add eggs and knead until a smooth ball. If dough is too soft, gradually add a little flour. Divide dough in 4 pieces, roll each piece to 1/4" thickness on floured board. Cut with pastry cutter into thin strips, 6" long and 1" wide, tie into a loose knot. Deep fry until golden brown, drain and sprinkle with confectioners sugar.

Josephine Furnari
Charles J. Bonaparte Lodge #2504
Rose Malzone
Ft. Lauderdale Lodge #2263

Variation
6 cups flour
1/2 cup lard, softened
2 tbsp. baking powder
oil for frying

6 eggs
1/4 cup sugar
1 tsp. salt
1 cup confectioners sugar

Follow blending and kneading directions above. Cut dough into strips, tie into a knot. Fry then drain on paper towels. Cool and sprinkle with powdered sugar.

Palma Guarante
Coral Springs Lodge #2332

Crispelle
(Fried Rosettes)

6 cups flour
oil for frying

6 eggs
1 jar honey

Make a well in the flour and add eggs one at a time working dough into a smooth ball. Cut dough into 4 pieces. Roll each piece to 1/4" thickness. If you have a macaroni machine, roll out to next to last notch. Cut dough into strips 3-4" long with a fluted pastry wheel pinching the "Rosette" in 3-4 spots so it will hold together. Fry in hot oil, *Do Not Crowd,* until golden brown. Drain on brown paper bag and let cool. Pour honey over top to serve.

Edith Cuccinelli
Sgt. F. M. Bonanno Lodge #2549

Crispelle
(Fried Rosettes)
continued

Variation: A very large recipe for festive occasions

2 dozen eggs	2 tsp. salt
4 tbsp. shortening	4 tbsp. sugar
(melted and cooled)	15 cups flour
2 tsp. baking powder	1 cup walnuts, chopped
1 tsp. baking soda	oil for frying
1 jar honey	

Follow directions on preceding page, adding all ingredients into flour well.

When 'Crispelle' are cooled, drizzle honey and walnuts over top.

Origin: My mother, Sabastianina Carozzulo, from Foggia, Italy.

Mary A. Sorci
John Paul I Lodge #2427

Biscotto
(Italian Cake)

4 eggs	4 tsp. baking powder
1 1/2 cups sugar	1 tsp. lemon rind, grated
1/4 cup butter, softened	2 1/2-3 cups flour
2 tsp. vanilla	1 egg yolk, beaten
1 cup raisins, optional	

Mix butter and sugar, beat 1 minute. Add eggs, vanilla and lemon rind, beating 2-3 minutes more. Add baking powder to 2 1/2 cups of flour and blend into eggs. Add raisins. Add more flour if cake dough seems too moist. This is a dense cake.

Pour into a greased floured tube pan. Brush top of dough with egg yolk to give a shiny finish. Bake in preheated oven 350 degrees for 30 minutes, lower heat to 325 degrees and bake another 30 minutes until golden brown. *(I bake my cake in a greased 10" iron skillet, with an oiled wine glass in the middle, then pour the batter around the glass.)*

To vary flavor, you may use 3 tsp. of anise or 1 tsp. of almond flavoring.

This type of cake is usually dunked in wine or coffee - enjoy.

Florence Santi
John Paul I Lodge #2427

Sponge Cake
(Cream-filled)

6 large eggs, room temperature   1 tsp. baking powder
6 rounded tbsp. sugar   1 tsp. vanilla extract
6 rounded tbsp. flour

In a mixer, beat eggs and 1 tablespoon of sugar at a time for about 15 minutes or until mixture becomes very thick and glossy.

Put flour and baking powder into a hand sifter. Sift flour into eggs, using a slotted spoon to fold in flour very gently. **Do not mix or stir.** Pour batter into a lightly greased and floured 10" round cake pan at least 3" deep. Shake pan slightly to even batter out. Bake in a preheated 325 degree oven for 15-20 minutes until light golden color and edges leave pan. Invert cake onto a rack and let cool. Remove gently from pan. Cut cake into thirds or in half with a sharp knife.

Cream Filling
1 qt. warm milk   1 cup flour
2 whole eggs, beaten   2 cups sugar
1 tsp. vanilla extract

Mix flour and sugar. Slowly stir in milk and cook in a double boiler 15 minutes or until thick. Add a little hot mixture to eggs. Stir into remaining hot mixture. Continue cooking 3 minutes; add vanilla and cool.

(To make chocolate cream, add 1/2 cocoa to flour and sugar blending well before the milk is added).

Whipped Cream Frosting
3 (1/2 pts.) heavy whipping cream
3 tbsp. confectioners sugar

Pour heavy cream into a cold mixing bowl. Add powdered sugar and whip until thick enough to frost the cake. (Be careful not to over beat - you will break cream down and make sweet butter.) I cover cream filled cake layer with sliced sugared strawberries, then decorate the top with whole strawberries. My family prefers one layer chocolate and one vanilla and then frosted all over with whipped cream. The cake tastes better and serves easier if made early in the day and has time to moisten. This cake can be made ahead and frozen. Fill layers with cream then wrap in Saran wrap. Frost with whipped cream 3-4 hours before you serve. Traditional to our family for all birthdays and festive occasions.

Origin: Grandma, Rosina Boniello

Rose Marie Boniello
Sgt. F. M. Bonanno Lodge #2549

Torta di Cioccolata
(Chocolate Covered Sponge Cake)

4 eggs, separated
1/4 cup sugar
1/4 cup cornstarch, sifted
8 oz. semi-sweet chocolate
   (chopped)

pinch of salt
1/2 tsp. vanilla extract
1/4 cup flour, sifted
1/4 cup rum

Grease a 1" x 10" x 15" cookie sheet and line with wax paper. Grease and flour wax paper. Beat egg whites with salt until they hold soft peaks. Gradually beat in sugar, sprinkling it in 1 tablespoon at a time. Continue beating until whites are very firm about 5 minutes. Stir yolks with a fork to break them up. Add vanilla, fold 1/4 of the stiffly beaten egg whites thoroughly into egg yolk, then fold remaining egg whites. Sprinkle cornstarch and flour on top, fold very gently together until egg white is blended. Be careful not to over mix.

Pour into prepared pan. Spread batter evenly, bake in preheated hot oven 400 degrees, 10-12 minutes or until cake is very lightly browned. **Be careful not to over bake.** Loosen sides and remove cake from pan at once. Cool on a rack before peeling off paper. Cake should be flexible from end to end. Cut cake in half , then split each layer to make 3 layers. Sprinkle each layer with rum and top with the filling, alternate the white cream filling with the chocolate. Melt chocolate in a double boiler or microwave oven. Cool chocolate slightly then cover the top and the sides of the cake. Refrigerate.

Butter Cream Filling
3 eggs
1 lb. butter, room temperature
1/4 cup cocoa

1 1/4 cup sugar
2 1/2 tsp. vanilla extract

Put eggs and sugar on top of the stove to warm up, then beat the mixture in a blender, adding the butter a little at a time to a pudding consistency. Add vanilla. Divide cream in thirds. Use white cream filling for two layers of the cake. Add cocoa to remaining cream and spread on third layer.

Renata Curcio Rathmann
La Nuova Sicilia #1251

Italian Raisin Cake

1 1/2 cups water
1 cup raisins
1 1/2 tsp. baking soda
3 eggs, beaten
2 cups sugar

1 tsp. vanilla
1 1/2 tsp. salt
3 cups flour
1 cup oil
1 cup walnuts, chopped

Boil water and raisins, remove from heat, add baking soda, cool and set aside. Add sugar, vanilla, and salt to eggs. Beat until well blended. Mix eggs slowly into flour, then add oil and raisins with the water. Mix well, then fold in walnuts.

Flour and grease a spring form tube pan, pour in cake batter and bake in a preheated 350 degree oven for one hour. Center will be slightly moist. Cake stays fresh for one week and can also be frozen.

Flo Carbone
Sunrise-Tamarac Lodge #2542

Italian Cheese Cake

2 (8 oz.) pkgs. cream cheese
1 lb. ricotta cheese
1 1/4 cups sugar
4 eggs, beaten
3 tbsp. flour
3 tbsp. cornstarch

1 1/2 tbsp. lemon juice
1 tsp. lemon rind, grated
1 tsp. vanilla
1/2 cup butter, melted
1 pint sour cream

Graham Cracker Crust
11-12 Graham crackers crushed
fine
2 tbsp. sugar

1 cup butter or margarine
(melted)

Crust
Melt butter and pour over graham crackers. Add sugar, mix well. Spread evenly into a large buttered square cake pan. Bake 15 minutes, 325 degrees. Cool.

Cake batter
Beat the cream cheese with ricotta until well blended. Gradually beat in the sugar and eggs, then add cornstarch, flour, lemon juice, rind, and vanilla. Add butter and sour cream, beat until smooth. Pour into cake pan, bake 1 hour and 10 minutes until firm around the edges. Turn the oven off, let pan stand in the oven for 2 hours. Refrigerate for 3 hours before serving. Top with your favorite pie filling. I use blueberry on half, and strawberry on the other half.

Marie Runfola
Joseph A. Franzalia Lodge #2422

Ricotta Cheese Cake

1 (3 lb.) can ricotta
2 cups sugar
1/2 cup flour
1 tsp. vanilla
1 lemon and 1 orange rind, grated
1/2 cup graham cracker crumbs

8 eggs, separated
3 tbsp. anisette
3 tbsp. creme de cocoa
1/4 cup chocolate bits
1/2 cup whipped cream (optional)
2 tbsp. butter, softened

Beat ricotta until smooth, gradually adding 1 1/2 cups sugar and egg yolks. Add flour, vanilla, orange and lemon rind. Beat egg whites with 1/2 cup sugar. Fold whipped cream, egg whites and chocolate bits into the ricotta mixture. Turn into a 12" spring form pan which has been buttered and sprinkled with graham cracker crumbs. Bake in preheated oven 425 degrees for 10 minutes. Lower temperature to 350 degrees and bake 1 hour. Turn off heat and allow to cool in oven with door closed. Refrigerate.

Origin: Family recipe from my aunt.

Rose Malzone
Ft. Lauderdale Lodge #2263

Cannoli

Shell
1 1/3 cups flour
pinch of salt
white wine (sweet or dry)

1 tbsp. shortening
1/2 tsp. sugar
oil for frying

Mix flour, shortening, salt and sugar. Add enough wine to make a stiff workable dough. Roll into ball and let it stand for about 1 hour. Roll out dough 1/8" thick. Cut into 5" squares. Place cannoli tube across the corners of the square. Fold one corner around the tube, then the other and press together. Fry in deep oil, one at a time, until golden brown. Remove cannoli carefully and let cool before filling.

Ricotta Filling
1 lb. ricotta
1 tbsp. orange peel, cut fine
2 tbsp. sugar

2 tbsp. chocolate chips
2 1/2 tbsp. creme de cacao or
(any other liqueur)

Cream ricotta, add chocolate chips, orange peel, creme de cacao and sugar mixing well. Fill shells with filling. Sprinkle with confectioners sugar. Serves 12.

Rose Marie Tufarella
Sunrise-Tamarac Lodge #2542

Ricotta Pie
(Chocolate Marbled Filling)

Crust

3 cups flour
1 cup confectioners sugar
1/2 tsp. baking powder
1/2 tsp. vanilla

1/2 cup lard
2 egg yolks
1/4 cup water

Mix flour, sugar and baking powder. Cut lard into flour mixture. Add vanilla to egg yolks and blend in water. Add egg mixture to flour and mix well by hand. Roll out dough and line bottom of a 3 quart oblong pyrex dish. Save some dough for lattice strips.

Filling

3 lbs. ricotta
1 1/2 tsp. lemon extract
1 tbsp. vanilla
1 tbsp. diced citron, optional

l cup sugar
8 egg whites
1/8 tsp. salt

Beat egg whites until fluffy, blend in all other ingredients. Set to one side.

Melted chocolate

Melt 4 - 1 oz. squares of chocolate. Blend in 2 tablespoons sugar and 1 egg yolk. Set aside.

Pour half of the ricotta filling over crust. Drop chocolate with a teaspoon (randomly) over filling. Pour remaining ricotta filling over top. Swirl with a spoon to give a marbled effect.

Roll and cut remaining dough in strips and form a lattice top. Brush with egg white. Bake in preheated oven 350 degrees 1 hour.

M. Palma Guarente
Coral Springs Lodge #2332

Chocolate Ricotta Cheese Pie

3 cups ricotta cheese
1 cup sugar
4 eggs
1 cup heavy cream
1-10" pie crust shell

1/8 tsp. salt
1/3 cup unsweetened cocoa
1/4 cup flour
1/2 tsp. vanilla

Beat ricotta cheese, sugar and eggs in a blender. Add remaining ingredients, process until well blended. Pour into the pie shell. Bake in preheated 350 degree oven, 1 hour and 15 minutes until set. Turn oven off and let stand in oven, 1 hour. Refrigerate. Serve plain or topped with fruit and whipped cream.

Pauline Parker
Joseph A. Franzalia Lodge 2422

Tirami-Su
("Pick Me Up")

2 pkgs. Savoiardi Lady Fingers
10 eggs, separated
10 tbsp. sugar
2 cups expresso coffee, room
temperature

2 lbs. Mascarpone
(Italian cream cheese)
1 cup vermouth
2 tbsp. powdered semi-sweet
cocoa

Beat egg yolks and sugar together, add cream cheese and blend well. Beat egg whites until peaks form, then fold into cheese mixture.

In oblong baking dish, place a thin layer of cheese mixture. Mix coffee and vermouth, dip lady fingers in mixture and layer the bottom of the pan. Add a layer of cheese and sprinkle with cocoa. Continue with another layer, finishing with cocoa. Refrigerate 2 hours before serving.

Antonette Zaffarano
Sgt. F. M. Bonanno Lodge #2549

Variation
5 eggs
1 lb. ricotta
1 lb. 2 oz. Mascarpone
5 tbsp. rum
1 oz. grated chocolate

2 boxes Savoiardi Lady Fingers
2 tbsp. sugar
1 cup expresso coffee,
sweetened

Mix coffee and rum, blending ricotta, mascarpone, sugar and eggs together to form a cheese mixture. Follow instructions above ending with a layer of cheese. Sprinkle grated chocolate over top.

Renata Curcio Rathmann
La Nuova Scilia Lodge #1251

Ricotta Pie

Pie Crust

2 1/4 cups flour
2 tbsp. shortening
1/8 tsp. salt

1/4 cup sugar
2/3 cup hot water

Melt shortening in hot water, add sugar and mix well. Add salt and flour, continue to mix and form a ball of dough. Cover with a towel and let rest. Roll out dough to cover pie plate and crimp the edges. With the extra dough pieces, roll out strips to form a lattice top.

Filling

3 lbs. ricotta
3/4 cup sugar
1 tbsp. lemon rind, grated

6 large eggs
2 tsp. vanilla
10" pie plate, 2" deep

Cream ricotta, sugar and eggs with a mixer until well blended. Add vanilla and lemon rind. Pour into the crust lined pie plate. Bake in preheated oven at 350 degrees for 1 hour. Turn oven off and let set for 15 minutes. Remove and cool. Dust with confectioners sugar to serve.

Ellen C. Fiegenbaum
Ft. Lauderdale Lodge #2263

Variation
Add 1 tsp. orange rind grated, and two tbsp. each of lemon and orange juice to ricotta mixture.

Rose Marie Tufarella
Sunrise-Tamarac Lodge #2542

Variation
Omit lemon rind. Add 1 tsp. vanilla, 1/4 cup diced citron, 1 oz. grated chocolate or 1/4 cup chocolate bits and 1/4 cup chopped Maraschino cherries.

Jeanette D'Alessandro
Coral Springs Lodge #2332

Variation
Add 2 tbsp. each of lemon and orange rind, grated, and 1 tsp. vanilla.

Adeline Villano McNulty
Sons of Italy Lodge #321
Schenectady, New York

Biscotti di Vino
(Wine Biscuit)

2 1/2 cups unbleached flour
1 1/2 tsp. course grind pepper
1/2 cup dry red wine

1/3 cup sugar
1 1/2 tsp. baking powder
1/2 cup vegetable oil

In a food processor or mixer, blend flour, sugar, black pepper and baking powder. As mixer is running, add oil and wine slowly. Blend until the mixture forms a dough. Remove the dough and place on a board. Divide the dough into 30 pieces. Roll each piece into a 3" long rope and then press ends together to form a ring. Arrange rings 1 1/2" apart on an ungreased baking sheet. Bake in batches in the middle of the oven at 350 degrees for 20-30 minutes, or until bottoms are golden brown. Cool on a rack for 5 minutes. **"Suono Molti Buoni"**.

Rose Marie Boniello
Sgt. F. M. Bonanno Lodge #2549

Taralli

1/4 cup olive oil
4 cups flour

6 eggs, separated
1/8 tsp. baking soda

Beat eggs separately, yolks should be firm. Place flour on a board, make a well. Add yolks and whites a little at a time. Blend well and knead for about 10-15 minutes. Cut a piece of dough and roll into a pencil shape, 1/4" round by 6" long. Form into a circle and pinch the ends. Shape all the dough and place on a cloth covered surface.

Bring a large pot of water to a slow boil. Drop a few Taralli in the water at a time (do not crowd). Remove immediately as they surface. Place on a cloth and let dry 1 to 2 hours. Preheat oven to 500 degrees. Place Taralli on a cookie sheet and bake 20 minutes until they have raised and are golden in color.

Icing
1 cup confectioners sugar
water as needed

1 tbsp. lemon juice

Mix confectioners sugar, lemon juice and some water to form an icing. Frost Taralli while still warm.

Grayce DeBartolo
Sgt. F. M. Bonanno Lodge #2549

Pignolata
(Honey Clusters)

Dough

3 cups flour	1/8 tsp. baking powder
1 tbsp. margarine	1 tbsp. whiskey
6 eggs, beaten	oil for frying

Sugar Syrup

1 1/2 cups sugar	1 tbsp. honey

Work margarine into the flour and baking powder until thoroughly mixed. Add whiskey and eggs, knead the dough until smooth and firm. Form a ball of dough and cover. Cut a piece of dough and roll into a long thin rope, about 1/2" round. Cut pieces 5/8" long. Cut only enough dough to fry at one time.

Heat oil. The right temperature is reached when you drop a piece of dough and it floats to the top. Add Pignolata without crowding, stirring with a slotted spoon until golden brown. Remove and let drain in a colander. Transfer Pignolata to cool on a paper towel. Continue until all the dough is fried.

Melt sugar, stirring constantly until sugar turns golden brown. Add one tbsp. honey, stir quickly. Add the fried Pignolata, stirring until all the pieces are well coated. Working quickly, pour on to a formica cutting board. Wet hands with cold water (be careful, sugar can burn your hands), and quickly shape the pieces into a round dome. Immediately decorate with multi-colored sprinkles. Can be kept in the freezer in a plastic container for as long as a year.

Comment: Katie LaRocca, wife of one of our founders, Angelo LaRocca, received this recipe from her relative in Italy. It is used as one of the ethnic desserts sold at Fiesta Day in Ybor City, which is a part of the Gasparilla Celebration in Tampa, Florida.

Angie C. Demmi
Unita Lodge #2015

Pignolata/Strufoli

6 eggs
3 tbsp. margarine

3 cups flour
oil for frying
1 cup sugar

Cut margarine into flour, add eggs one at a time kneading dough until smooth. Cut off pieces of dough and roll about 1/4" in diameter. Cut into 1" pieces and fry in hot oil, stirring constantly until golden brown. Remove Pignolata to drain on a brown paper bag.

Melt 1 cup of sugar until golden brown. Add about 3 cups of Pignolata, stirring until kernels are coated. Remove from pan on to counter dampened with water and with wet hands, form Pignolata into 3" clusters.

Mary S. Settecasi
La Nuova Sicilia Lodge #1251

Strufoli/Pignolata
(Baked in the Oven)

Dough
3 1/2 - 4 cups flour
1 1/2 tsp. baking powder
1/4 cup sugar
1/4 tsp. salt

4 eggs, beaten
1/2 cup oil
1 tsp. vanilla

Honey Coating:
1/2 - 3/4 cup honey, warmed
colored sprinkles

1/4 cup citron, diced

Mix 3 1/2 cups of flour, baking powder, sugar and salt. Mix eggs, oil and vanilla. Add eggs to flour and work into a dough. Knead about 5 minutes or until smooth. Add more flour if needed. Cut off a piece of dough and roll into a rope about 1/2" round. Cut into 1" pieces. Put pieces of dough on to greased baking sheets. Bake in preheated oven 350 degrees until Struffoli are lightly browned.

Warm honey, add citron and pour over cooled Struffoli. Decorate with colored sprinkles.

Nancy DeGregory
Rev. Albert B. Palombo Lodge #2512

Strufoli/Pignolata
(Fried)

4-5 cups flour
2 tsp. baking powder
1 tsp. salt
3 tbsp. white wine
colored sprinkles
candied cherries

1/4 cup corn oil
6 eggs, beaten
1 1/2 lb. jar honey
1/2 cup pine nuts
   (pignoli)
oil for frying

Mix flour, baking powder and salt on a pastry board. Make a well, add wine, 1/4 cup oil and eggs, gradually blending ingredients with a fork. Mix to form a dough. Knead until smooth and soft. Cut dough in half. Roll each half into 1/4" thickness. Cut into 1/2" wide strips and roll each strip into a pencil shape. Cut pencil shape strips into 1/4" pieces. Heat oil to 350 degrees. Drop pieces into oil (do not crowd). Stir to brown lightly. Remove to paper towels and cool.

Simmer honey to 250 degrees on a candy thermometer or until a little honey dropped into cold water, forms a soft ball. Remove from heat, stir in pine nuts, pour over Strufoli, tossing to coat well. Top with sprinkles and candied cherries. *"A Christmas Treat"*.

"Scoogie" Fazzari
Submitted by Jean Boniello
Sgt. F. M. Bonanno Lodge #2549

Variation: Omit wine, add 1 tsp. vanilla.

Jeanette D'Alessandro
Coral Springs Lodge #2332

Variation: Omit wine, add 1 tbsp. anisette or almond extract.

Rose Malzone
Ft. Lauderdale Lodge #2263

Cenci
(Fried Sweet Pastry)

2 1/4 cups flour	2 eggs, slightly beaten
2 tbsp. rum or white wine	2 egg yolks
1 tbsp. confectioners sugar	1/8 tsp. salt

Place 2 cups of flour in a large bowl. Make a well, add eggs, yolks, rum, confectioners sugar and salt. Work to a very stiff but pliable dough. Knead well, using more flour if needed. Wrap in a cloth and let rest 1 hour in a cool place.

On a floured board, roll out one quarter of the dough (rather thin) to approximately 1/8" thickness. Cut into rectangles, 3" x 4 1/2". Make 3 lengthwise cuts into each rectangle. Tie the strips into loose knots. Fry the knots, 3 or 4 at a time, in hot oil until puffed and golden brown. Drain on paper towels. When cold, dust with confectioners sugar. Repeat until all dough is fried. Makes about 4 dozen.

Origin: My mother, Rosa Depascale Cellucci

Maria Cellucci Atkins
Key West Lodge #2436

Comment: My mother, aunt, and grandmother made these delicious pastries.

Rita J. Ricci
John Paul I Lodge #2427

Cassata alla Siciliano

2 lbs ricotta	1 cup sugar
1 tsp. vanilla	1/4 cup creme de cocoa (white)
1/2 cup mini chocolate chips	3 pkgs. Lady Fingers

Combine ricotta, sugar, vanilla and creme de cocoa. Beat for 10 minutes at medium speed. Stir in chocolate bits. Line a spring form pan with Lady Fingers, bottom and sides. Pour half of the filling in the pan. Cover filling with Lady Fingers. Pour remaining filling, followed by Lady Fingers. Refrigerate. Remove from pan just before serving.

Origin: My family

Vito J. Rossi
Charles J. Bonaparte Lodge #2504

Bocci di Ricotta
(Ricotta Fritters)

1 lb. ricotta	3/4 cup plain breadcrumbs
3 tbsp. sugar	1/8 tsp. cinnamon
1 egg	Bread crumbs for dredging
oil for frying	1 egg beaten with 1 tbsp. water.

Blend ricotta, sugar, eggs, 3/4 cup bread crumbs and cinnamon. Form into 24 balls. Roll in bread crumbs, egg and then in bread crumbs again. Deep fry in oil until golden brown. *Serve warm as a side dish or sprinkle with powdered sugar to serve with coffee.*

Origin: Family recipe by Zia Sarina.

Margaret Scarfia
John Paul I Lodge #2427

Sfingi di Ricotta
(Ricotta Puffs)

1 lb. ricotta	3 lg. eggs, slightly beaten
1 tbsp. sugar	1 cup flour
4 tsp. baking powder	2 tbsp. orange rind
1/8 tsp. salt	(finely chopped, optional)
1 tsp. vanilla	3 tbsp. rum or brandy
1/4 cup confectioners sugar	(optional)
oil for frying	

Combine ricotta, eggs and sugar. Add baking powder and salt to flour. Gradually add flour mixture to ricotta and beat well. Add vanilla, orange rind and rum. Cover and let rest a half hour.

Heat oil. Drop batter by the teaspoonful into hot oil. **Do not crowd.** If needed, turn Sfingi with a slotted spoon. When golden in color, remove and place on paper towels to drain. Serve, dusted with confectioners sugar.

Rose Van Saake
Sgt. F. M. Bonanno Lodge #2549
Grayce DeBartolo
Sgt. F. M. Bonanno Lodge #2549
Rita Ricci
John Paul I Lodge #2427

Comment: "Zeppole" is the name given to this delicious ricotta doughnut in my family.

Judy E. Terrana
Unita Lodge #2015

Cassatelle
(Fried Triangles of Dough Stuffed With Ricotta)

Dough

7 cups flour
1 cup shortening
1/2 tsp. salt
oil for frying

1/2 cup sugar
1 1/4 cups lukewarm water
l egg white beaten (reserve)

Cut shortening into flour and salt. Dissolve sugar in warm water and beat into flour to form a pie dough. Knead well, then cut into 4 pieces. Knead each piece again then cover and set aside for 1 hour.

Filling

3 lbs. ricotta
1/2 cup mini chocolate bits
1 tsp. cinnamon

l tsp. vanilla
1/2 cup sugar

Drain ricotta in a colander, cover and refrigerate for two days. Should feel dry to the touch. Mix all ingredients well and set aside.

Roll dough to l/8" thickness. Cut into 3 1/2" squares. Brush squares with egg white. Fill center with 1 tbsp. of ricotta, fold dough over to make a triangle. Seal edges with the tines of a fork. Prick top. Placed filled triangles on a floured cloth.

Heat oil. Place Cassatelle gently in hot oil. Do not crowd. When edges are gold in color, turn and carefully fry on other side. Remove, drain on paper towels. Dust with confectioners sugar to serve.

Origin: Traditional to my Sicilian family.

**Rose Van Saake
Sgt. F. M. Bonanno Lodge #2549**

Pizzelle
(Waffle Cookie)

1 1/2 cups sugar
3 large eggs
1/2 cup butter (melted)
1 tsp. vanilla or anise

2 cups flour
1 1/2 tsp. baking powder
1/8 tsp. salt

Beat together, sugar, eggs, butter and vanilla. Add flour, baking powder, salt and mix well. The dough should be sticky enough to be dropped from a spoon. Heat Pizzelle electric iron (7-8 minutes) and drop 1 heaping teaspoon of batter on each Pizzelle form. Bake 30 seconds until golden brown and crisp.

**Virginia Papale
Sunrise-Tamarac Lodge #2542
Fiore and Idoni
Key West Lodge #2436**

Honey Cakes

1 cup corn oil	4 cups flour
1 cup white wine	1 tsp. cinnamon
(muscatel or sherry)	oil for frying

Mix oil and wine, bring to a boil and let cool. Add cinnamon to flour in a large bowl. Make a well and add cooled liquid slowly, working with your fingers to form a soft pliable dough. Break off pieces of dough and roll into long thin rope. Cut into 1"pieces, roll gently on a grooved board or make ridges with the tines of a fork. Drop the "cakes" in hot oil a few at a time and fry until golden. Drain on brown paper. When cool, pour honey over top. *"A special treat at Christmas Time."*

Origin: Americo and Clara Testa

Barbara Testa
Lake Worth/Boynton Beach Lodge #2304

Variation: Honey syrup
1 tablespoon sugar for each cup of honey. Boil for 5 minutes. When "cookies" or cakes are cool, coat in hot syrup. Sprinkle confettini over top. *My mom called this recipe "sweet cookies" and served them at Christmas time.*

Origin: My mother

Rose Malzone
Ft. Lauderdale Lodge #2263

Biscotti alla Rose Marie

1 cup margarine, softened	4 cups flour
1 3/4 cups sugar	6 tsp. baking powder
6 eggs	1 oz. anise flavoring

In a mixer, cream margarine and sugar. Add eggs and anise flavoring, continue to beat for 1-2 minutes. Mix flour and baking powder. Add flour to eggs on low speed, until well blended.

Dough will be a firm cake batter consistency. Drop dough by the tablespoonful onto a greased cookie sheet. Shape dough into a loaf with two knives. The batter makes 4 loaves. Bake 325 degrees for 25 minutes until a light tan in color. Loaves will be cooked but soft.

Remove carefully with a spatula and cut into 3/4" diagonal slices. Return to a 350 degree oven and bake slices to a golden brown. Biscotti will keep for several weeks in a tightly closed metal can, lined with paper towel.

Rose Marie Boniello
Sgt. F. M. Bonanno Lodge #2549

Rice Casata

1 cup rice	1 cup citron, chopped
6 eggs	6 oz. chocolate chips
1 1/2 cups sugar	1 tsp. vanilla
2 lbs. ricotta	1/4 tsp. cinnamon

Cook rice in 2 1/2 cups of water. Let cool. Beat eggs, sugar and ricotta until light and creamy. Add rice mixing well. Add citron, chocolate chips, vanilla and cinnamon. Stir to blend all ingredients. Pour into an oblong pyrex dish.

Bake in a low oven, 275 degrees for 2 hours.

Elisa Santucci
Joseph A. Franzalia Lodge #2422

Panelle
(A Sicilian Treat)

4 cups chickpea flour (ceci)	1 tsp. salt
6 cups water	oil for frying

Put chickpea flour in a saucepan and add water very slowly, stirring carefully to avoid lumps. Add salt, cover over medium heat, stir constantly about 15 minutes until mixture is very thick.

Pour mixture onto a lightly oiled marble or wooden surface and spread it out quickly with an oiled spatula into a thin sheet, 1/4" thick. When cool cut into 2"X3" rectangles.

Fry the panelle in hot oil, a few at a time, turn once until both sides are golden brown. Drain on paper towel, serve hot. This tasty treat was served in celebration of "Santa Lucia" (St. Lucy's Day).

Origin: Laura and Anthony Massa

Barbara Testa
Lake Worth/Boynton Beach Lodge #2304

Easter Wheat Pie

2 cups flour, sifted   1/4 cup butter
1/2 cup sugar   3 egg yolks
pinch of salt   1 tbsp. milk

Mix flour, salt and sugar. Cut in butter evenly through flour mixture. Stir
in egg yolks one at a time. Work until dough is manageable. Add milk.
Turn onto a lightly floured board and knead until smooth. Form into a ball
and chill for 30 minutes. Divide the ball in half, roll on lightly floured
board to about 1/8" thick (large enough to line a deep 10" pie plate).
Butter pie plate and line with pastry, leaving 1/2" overhang. Roll out other
piece of dough and cut into 3/4" strips for lattice topping.

Filling

1 can wheat   1 1/2 lbs. ricotta
1/4 cup milk, scalded   1 cup sugar
1/4 tsp. salt   6 eggs, separated
1/4 tsp. sugar   1 tbsp. orange water
1/4 cup citron, diced   1 tsp. vanilla
   (optional)   2 tbsp. confectioners sugar
1/4 orange peel, diced

In the scalded milk, mix wheat, salt and sugar. Boil for 5 minutes.
Remove from heat, add citron and orange peel, set aside. To prepare
filling, beat ricotta and sugar, then add egg yolks, vanilla and orange
water, blend well. Stir in prepared wheat and fold in beaten egg whites.
Pour into pie shell. Arrange lattice topping over filling, flute the edge.
Bake in preheated 350 degree oven for 1 hour or until firm in center. Let
cool in oven with door open. Refrigerate. To serve dust with
confectioners sugar.

Renata Curcio Rathmann
La Nuova Sicilia Lodge #1251
Eleanor Bruno
John Paul I Lodge #2427
Vito J. Rossi
Charles J. Bonaparte Lodge #2504

Editor's Note: Wheat (grano) can be purchased by the ounce in an Italian
   Specialty Market. For this recipe use 2 1/2 ounces or 1/2 cup.
   Simmer grano with 1 cup water and the peeled rind of one orange to
   a barley form, 30 to 35 minutes. Cook, drain, and use in the above
   recipe.

Sfingi
(Sicilian Cream Puffs/Sfingi di San Guiseppe)

1/2 cup butter or margarine
1 cup boiling water
1/8 tsp. salt

4 eggs
1 cup flour

Put butter and water in a saucepan. Bring to a boiling point. Mix flour and salt, add all at once. Mix well, stirring constantly until mixture is smooth and shiny, and leaves the side of the pan. Remove from heat. Add whole eggs, one at a time, beating vigorously after each egg. Drop a teaspoon full of batter on greased baking sheet, spaced 2" apart. Bake at 400 degrees for 35 minutes or until nicely browned. Remove puffs and cool.

Ricotta Filling:
1 lb. ricotta cheese
1/4 tsp. almond extract
1/2 cup sugar

2 oz. unsweetened chocolate (grated)

Combine ricotta and sugar, mixing well. Stir in grated chocolate and almond extract. When cool, cut side of each puff. Fill with ricotta filling. Makes 24 puffs.

Diana Durso
Mike Accardi Lodge #2441

Bianco Mangiare
(Pudding)

2 tbsp. sugar
2 tbsp. cornstarch
2 cups whole milk
1/4 cup chocolate chips

1 pkg. Lady Fingers (or 9" sponge cake)
4 tbsp. rum
candied cherries

Dissolve cornstarch in 1/4 cup of milk and set aside. Heat remaining milk over low heat, add sugar stirring to dissolve. DO NOT BOIL. Using a wooden spoon, add dissolved cornstarch, stirring constantly *in one direction* on medium heat until milk thickens to a pudding consistency. Remove from heat, let cool slightly.

Line a platter with Lady Fingers and sprinkle with rum. Pour thick cream over top. Decorate with chocolate chips and candied cherries. Refrigerate 2 hours before serving.

Origin: Traditional to my family.

Rose Van Saake
Sgt. F. M. Bonanno Lodge #2549

Cuddureddi
(Fig Rings)

2 whole orange peelings   3 cups water
2 cups sugar

Boil water, sugar and orange peelings about 15 minutes. Set aside.

Filling
3 lbs. dry figs   1 lb. shelled almonds, roasted
3/4 cup sherry wine   1 tsp. nutmeg
1 tsp. cinnamon   1 tsp. black pepper

Cut figs into quarters, remove stems. Add boiled orange peelings and water, soak overnight.

Dough
12 cups flour   1 tsp. salt
1 1/2 cups shortening   2 cups sugar
water as needed

Cut shortening into flour, add sugar and salt. Add water to make a workable pie dough consistency. Knead dough until smooth. Roll into a ball, cover let rest about an hour. Roll dough into a square piece to 1/8" thickness and 12" long. Cut strips 2 3/4" wide and 12" long. Spread fig mixture in the center of each strip (about the size of a thumb). Bring the long edges of the dough together and seal. Cut filled dough in half. Form each piece into a ring and tuck the ends under. With a pair of scissors snip the top of the ring in several places, brush with a beaten egg yolk. Continue with remaining strips. Place on a greased cookie sheet about 1" apart. Bake in a preheated oven 325 degrees about 20 minutes or until dough is golden brown.

> *My grandmother brought this old recipe from Italy and made these fig rings for Christmas and for St. Joseph's Feast. The recipe has been handed down for four generations and I am the only one that continues this tradition in my family.*

> Angie C. Demmi
> Unita Lodge #2015

Neppetelle
(Calabrese Easter Cookie)

Filling
1 1/2 cups raisins, soaked   1 tsp. cloves
2 lbs. shelled walnuts, chopped   1 1/4 cup sugar
18 oz. jar cherry jam   8 oz. vino cotto or
2 tsp. cinnamon   (1 cup grape jelly)
1/4 cup cocoa

continued on next page

Neppetelle
(Calabrese Easter Cookie)
continued

Drain raisins and squeeze dry. Add raisins and all of the above ingredients into a large sauce pan and cook slowly until thickened. Set aside to cool.

Pastry Dough

8 cups flour
1/2 cup sugar
8 tbsp. oil

1 lemon rind, grated
2 pkgs. dry yeast
milk (as needed)

Work all ingredients together to form a dough, adding some milk as needed. Knead mixture a minute or two. Roll small pieces of dough into a 2 1/2"-3" circle. Fill each half with a tablespoon of filling, fold over like a turnover. Bake in a preheated oven 300 degrees until golden brown. Test with a toothpick if filling is dry.

This was my mother's favorite recipe handed down to her by Zia Concettina who was born in the 1800's. My older sister and I cracked the walnuts and chopped them, helping my mother to prepare for Easter baking.

Renata Curcio Rathmann
La Nuova Sicilia Lodge #1251

"Chialies"
(Filled Cookie for Easter)

4 cups flour
1 tsp. baking powder
2 tbsp. butter, softened
oil for frying

8 tsp. sugar
4 eggs
1 tsp. vanilla

Mix flour and baking powder. Cut in butter, then add sugar, eggs and vanilla. Work the mixture into a pliable dough. Set aside

Filling

2 cups walnuts, chopped fine
3/4-1 cup honey

8 oz. sweet German chocolate
(grated)

Mix walnuts and chocolate, add honey a little at a time to form a firm paste. Roll dough to 1/4" thickness. Cut into 3-4" circles. Place 1 tablespoon of filling on each circle, fold over to make a half moon shape. Seal the edges with the tines of a fork. Fry in hot oil until golden brown.

My brother and I were very young when my mother died but I remember helping her make these cookies for Easter. I shelled the walnuts and my brother would crush them with a hammer. These cookies are special to me and bring back fond childhood memories.

Origin: My mother Mary Mirabella, Calabria, Italy

Jean Boniello
Sgt. F. M. Bonanno Lodge #2549

Dolce di Ricotta al Gelato
(Frozen Ricotta Dessert)

5 eggs, separated
1 1/2 lbs. ricotta
2 cups sugar
1 1/2 cups Expresso coffee
(room temperature)

2 pkg. Lady Fingers
1 cup Galiano liqueur
1/2 cup water
1/2 cup chocolate bits

With a wire whisk, whip egg yolks, sugar and ricotta until creamy. In a separate bowl, whip egg whites with a blender until peaks form. Fold into ricotta mixture.

Dip Lady Fingers in coffee and layer bottom of a 9" X 12" baking pan. Pour 1/2 of the ricotta mixture over Lady Fingers. Combine Galiano and water. Dip next layer of Lady Fingers in Galiano. Pour remaining ricotta over top and cover with chocolate bits. Freeze for 2 hours before serving.

"A great make ahead dessert".

Antonette Zaffarano
Sgt. F. M. Bonanno Lodge #2549

Gelato Zabaglione

8 egg yolks
1/2 cup marsala or sherry wine
2 cups vanilla ice cream, softened
(more if preferred)

8 tsp. sugar
1 tbsp. brandy or rum

In top of double boiler beat egg yolks and sugar with an electric hand beater or wire whisk until mixture is light and frothy. Add marsala and brandy gradually while beating.

Place pan over hot simmering water and cook mixture, beating constantly until it begins to thicken. Remove from heat as soon as first bubbles appear and continue stirring until cool. Add ice cream and blend well. Freeze for several hours before serving. Serves 6-8.

Tradizione Italiana, per le feste natalizie, (ricetta vecchia). An old traditional recipe used for the Christmas holidays.

Pina DeFillippis
Sgt. F. M. Bonanno Lodge #2549

Panettone Farcito
(Stuffed Panettone)

2 lb. Panettone
1/4 cup amaretto, optional
1/4 cup sugar
1/4 cup heavy cream

1/2 cup maraschino juice
4 egg yolks
3/4 lb. mascarpone cheese

Slice the domed top from the panettone to form a cover.

Make a shell from the bottom leaving 1" sides and bottom. Cut the removed center into 1" cubes. Set aside. Sprinkle the shell with the combined maraschino juice and amaretto.

Beat egg yolks, sugar and mascarpone cheese until well blended. In a separate bowl beat cream until peaks form then fold into cheese mixture and refrigerate for 1 1/2 hours. Blend in panettone cubes and fill the shell. Replace dome top. Panettone may be covered with whipped cream or drizzled with chocolate. Refrigerate 2 hours before serving.

Comment: This dessert is great served at Christmas.

Antonette Zaffarano
Sgt. F. M. Bonanno Lodge #2549

Montagna Bianca
(Riced Chestnuts with Whipped Cream)

1 lb. chestnuts
1 pt. heavy cream
1 tsp. vanilla

1 1/2 tbsp. sweet liqueur
2 tbsp. confectioners sugar
1/2 cup nuts, chopped
(walnuts or pecans)

Place small cut on flat side of chestnuts, cover with water and boil for 30 minutes. Drain, peel and remove second skin while chestnuts are still warm. Put through ricer onto a serving platter with 1" or 2" edge. Form a mound, do not mash or press down, drizzle with liqueur. Refrigerate.

Beat heavy cream until peaks form. Add sugar and vanilla after you have started to beat. Top cold chestnut mound with enough whipped cream to look like a snow capped mountain. Sprinkle nuts over cream and refrigerate until served onto individual dessert dishes. "Godere" (enjoy).

Origin: Old family recipe.

Veni Hausold
Federico Tesio Lodge #2619

Ciliege Sotto Spirito
(Preserved Cherries)

1 1/2 lbs. Bing cherries	**2 cups Canadian Club whiskey**
1 qt. jar (sterilized)	

Buy cherries that are firm without blemishes and fresh enough so their stems are still green. Wash cherries, spread them out on a towel to dry. Remove stems and pack into the jar. Cover with whiskey, gently packing cherries to remove any trapped air. Completely cover cherries. Seal and refrigerate 4 weeks before serving.

Note: If you prefer to use Vodka, add a 1/2 cup of sugar, 3-4 whole cloves and piece of cinnamon stick. **Do no Stir.**

On special occasions and the holidays, my father served 3-4 cherries in a tiny whiskey glass with a little of the cherry liqueur. Our family continues this tradition to this day.

Origin: My father, Raul Giuliani

Rose Marie Boniello
Sgt. F. M. Bonanno Lodge #2549

Vino Cotto
"Cooked" Wine

20-30 lbs. sweet black grapes

Method
Crush grapes to extract liquid. Strain and measure the liquid extracted. Bring liquid to a rapid boil and quickly remove foam as it forms with a stainless steel spoon.

When liquid is clear, lower heat so it's boiling slowly. Reduce liquid to 1/3 of original measurement.

One hour before removing liquid from heat (*), fold in 2 apples (cut in quarters, seeds removed and cored) and 1 persimmon (cut in quarters).

(* Check consistency by spooning small portion in a plate. Liquid should now be about the thickness of maple syrup).

Ordinary table wine can not be used.

Origin: Zia Luiza Serino

John Boniello
Sgt. F. M. Bonanno Lodge #2549

ANTIPASTI
(Appetizers)

MINESTRE
(Soup)

MINESTRE (cont'd)
(Soup)

PANE E PIZZE
(Bread and Pizza)

PANE E PIZZE (cont'd)
(Bread and Pizza)

LE UOVA
(Eggs)

PRIMI PIATTI\FIRST COURSES
SALSE, PASTA, RISO, POLENTA
(Sauce, Pasta, Rice, Polenta)

PRIMI PIATTI\FIRST COURSES (cont'd)
SALSE, PASTA, RISO, POLENTA
(Sauce, Pasta, Rice, Polenta)

PRIMI PIATTI\FIRST COURSES (cont'd)
SALSE, PASTA, RISO, POLENTA
(Sauce, Pasta, Rice, Polenta)

SECONDI PIATTI\SECOND COURSES
CARNE, PESCE, POLLO
(Meat, Fish, Chicken)

MEAT

SECONDI PIATTI\SECOND COURSES
CARNE, PESCE, POLLO
(Meat, Fish, Chicken)

MEAT (cont'd)

**SECONDI PIATTI\SECOND COURSES
CARNE, PESCE, POLLO
(Meat, Fish, Chicken)**

MEAT (cont'd)

SECONDI PIATTI\SECOND COURSES
CARNE, PESCE, POLLO
(Meat, Fish, Chicken)

CHICKEN (cont'd)

CONTORNI
(Salads and Vegetables)

SALADS

VEGETABLES

CONTORNI
(Salads and Vegetables)

VEGETABLES (cont'd)

CONTORNI
(Salads and Vegetables)

VEGETABLES (cont'd)

DOLCI
(Desserts)

DOLCI (cont'd)
(Desserts)

DOLCI (cont'd)
(Desserts)

Preserving Our Italian Heritage
Sons of Italy Florida Foundation
87 NE 44th St., Ste. 5
Ft. Lauderdale, FL 33334

Please send me _____ copies of ***Preserving Our Italian Heritage*** at
$14.95 per copy plus $3.00 per book for postage and handling.
Enclosed is my check or money order for $ _____ .

Name_____

Address _____

City _____ State _____ Zip _____

Make check payable to Sons of Italy Florida Foundation.
Allow 2 - 3 weeks for delivery.

— —

Preserving Our Italian Heritage
Sons of Italy Florida Foundation
87 NE 44th St., Ste. 5
Ft. Lauderdale, FL 33334

Please send me _____ copies of ***Preserving Our Italian Heritage*** at
$14.95 per copy plus $3.00 per book for postage and handling.
Enclosed is my check or money order for $ _____ .

Name_____

Address _____

City _____ State _____ Zip _____

Make check payable to Sons of Italy Florida Foundation.
Allow 2 - 3 weeks for delivery.

— —

Preserving Our Italian Heritage
Sons of Italy Florida Foundation
87 NE 44th St., Ste. 5
Ft. Lauderdale, FL 33334

Please send me _____ copies of ***Preserving Our Italian Heritage*** at
$14.95 per copy plus $3.00 per book for postage and handling.
Enclosed is my check or money order for $ _____ .

Name_____

Address _____

City _____ State _____ Zip _____

Make check payable to Sons of Italy Florida Foundation.
Allow 2 - 3 weeks for delivery.

— —

53 EASTER BREAD RING 49-
182 ANISETTE COOKIES
139 CHICKEN AND SAUSAGE